IN
AMERICAN
HISTORY

THE UNION AND THE CIVIL WAR IN AMERICAN HISTORY

Mary E. Hull

Enslow Publishers, Inc.

40 Industrial Road   PO Box 38
Box 398   Aldershot
Berkeley Heights, NJ 07922 Hants GU12 6BP
USA   UK

http://www.enslow.com

This book is dedicated to Samuel F. Hull,
Solomon Stocker, and Stephen J. Wentworth.

Library of Congress Cataloging-in-Publication Data

Hull, Mary E.
    The Union and the Civil War in American history / Mary E. Hull.
       p. cm. — (In American history)
    Includes bibliographical references (p.) and index.
    Summary: Examines the contributions of soldiers, government officials,
free blacks, abolitionists, women, and children to the Union cause during
the Civil War.
    ISBN 0-7660-1416-9
    1. United States—History—Civil War, 1861–1865—Social aspects—
Juvenile literature. 2. United States—Politics and government—
1861–1865—Juvenile literature. [1. United States—History—Civil War,
1861–1865.] I. Title. II. Series.

E468.9 .H85 2000
973.7'1—dc21

                            99-041954

Printed in the United States of America

10 9 8 7 6 5 4 3 2

To Our Readers: We have done our best to make sure all Internet addresses in
this book were active and appropriate when we went to press. However, the
author and the publisher have no control over and assume no liability for the
material available on those Internet sites or on other Web sites they may link to.
Any comments or suggestions can be sent by e-mail to comments@enslow.com or
to the address on the back cover.

Illustration Credits: Courtesy of Mary E. Hull, p. 112; Enslow
Publishers, Inc., pp. 36, 47, 59, 96; Hugh Craig, *Grand Army Picture
Book* (New York: George Routledge and Sons, 1890), p. 12; Library of
Congress, pp. 7, 17, 26, 50; Mathew Brady et al., *Civil War Military
Leaders in Photographs* (New York: Dover Publications, Inc., 1998),
pp. 56, 62; Roy Meredith, *Mr. Lincoln's Camera Man: Mathew B. Brady*,
2nd Rev. ed. (New York: Dover Publications, Inc., 1974), pp. 54, 60,
80, 95, 102, 108; National Archives, pp. 6, 11, 29, 45, 65, 72, 77, 91,
99, 115.

Cover Illustration: National Archives; Roy Meredith, *Mr. Lincoln's
Camera Man: Mathew B. Brady*, 2nd Rev. ed. (New York: Dover
Publications, Inc., 1974).

★ CONTENTS ★

WAR!

On April 12, 1861, Confederate militiamen began firing on Fort Sumter in Charleston Harbor, South Carolina. The federal troops inside the fort were forced to surrender two days later, on April 14, 1861. This Confederate attack on the United States was an attempt to settle a long-standing argument over who had more power, the individual states or the federal government—an argument that had been made worse by Northern and Southern disagreement over slavery. After capturing Fort Sumter, Confederates tore down the American flag that had flown over the fort and raised their own flag of stars and bars.

News of Fort Sumter's fall to the Confederates spread rapidly. In the North, angry citizens held mass meetings to discuss what should be done. United States President Abraham Lincoln called on all the states to send seventy-five thousand militiamen to Washington, D.C. All the volunteers were asked to serve for ninety days in order to help put down what Lincoln called the Southern rebellion.

In the Northern half of the country, men rushed at this opportunity to fight for the preservation of their

The Civil War began when the Confederates fired on Fort Sumter, seen here just after the attack, flying the Confederate flag.

nation and the Constitution. Outraged by Lincoln's call for troops, more Southern states decided to withdraw from the Union and join the Confederacy. Southern men joined the Confederate Army in droves to defend their territory against what they considered Northern aggression. Citizens in both the North and the South prepared themselves for a war they believed would quickly be over.

Forming an Army

At the time of the attack on Fort Sumter in 1861, the United States Army consisted of fewer than seventeen thousand men. Most of them were scattered across the

Head Quarters, Virginia Forces,

STAUNTON, VA.

MEN OF VIRGINIA, TO THE RESCUE!

Your soil has been invaded by your Abolition foes, and we call upon you to rally at once, and drive them back. We want Volunteers to march immediately to Grafton and report for duty. Come one! Come ALL! and render the service due to your State and Country. Fly to arms, and succour your brave brothers who are now in the field.

The Volunteers from the Counties of Pendleton, Highland, Bath, Alleghany, Monroe, Mercer, and other Counties convenient to that point, will immediately organize, and report at Monterey, in Highland County, where they will join the Companies from the Valley, marching to Grafton. The Volunteers from the Counties of Hardy, Hampshire, Randolph, Pocahontas, Greenbrier, and other Counties convenient, will in like manner report at Beverly. And the Volunteers from the Counties of Upshur, Lewis, Barbour, and other Counties, will report at Philippi, in Barbour County. The Volunteers, as soon as they report at the above points, will be furnished with arms, rations, &c.,

Action! Action! should be our rallying motto, and the sentiment of Virginia's inspired Orator, "Give me Liberty or give me Death." animate every loyal son of the Old Dominion! Let us drive back the invading foot of a brutal and desperate foe. or leave a record to posterity that we died bravely defending our homes and firesides,—the honor of our wives and daughters,—and the sacred graves of our ancestors!

[Done by Authority.]

M. G. HARMAN, Maj. Commd'g
at Staunton.
J. M. HECK, Lt. Col. Va. Vol.
R. E. COWAN, Maj. Va. Vol.

May 30, 1861.

Responding with great anger to President Lincoln's call for troops, the Southern states that had seceded put out their own calls for volunteers to face the growing military crisis.

western territories. The United States did not have a large standing army, and it had not fought a war since the conflict with Mexico in 1846. Some towns still maintained volunteer militias, but most of the men were inexperienced. After the attack on Fort Sumter, towns rushed to create strong standing militias.

Young men who had never seen a battle joined their local militia and formed a company of volunteers. Companies from one town were joined with companies from nearby towns to create a unit of ten one-hundred-man companies, called a regiment. Each state regiment was numbered in the order in which it was accepted.

Men who volunteered to join the Union Army met on town greens, city squares, and at state militia camps. Without experience or uniforms, and sometimes even lacking weapons, they began drilling as a company of soldiers. The volunteers came from all backgrounds. Half of all the Union soldiers who served in the Civil War were farmers or the sons of farmers. The other half represented practically every occupation. Schoolteachers, ministers, clerks, mariners, tradesmen of all kinds, laborers, and college students all joined the war effort. One fourth of the men were recent immigrants from places such as Germany and Ireland.

In Union towns, citizens supported the war effort and encouraged their volunteers, sometimes traveling to the state militia camps to watch the regiments drill. In the North, ministers denounced secession and parishioners cheered for the Union soldiers, singing patriotic hymns. In an atmosphere of great excitement, people came out to bid farewell to the volunteers as they boarded the trains and steamships that would take them to the nation's capital. Their departure was celebrated. Orators delivered patriotic speeches, bands played military music, and public spaces were swathed with red, white, and blue bunting. Sometimes local women presented the regiments with a hand-sewn battle flag to carry. As the volunteers traveled away from their homes, they received a warm greeting at every Northern train station they passed. Crowds waved at them and raised enthusiastic cheers.

One of the first Union regiments to depart for Washington, D.C., was the 6th Massachusetts. Just one week after the attack on Fort Sumter, this regiment had already organized and was on its way to the nation's capital. On April 19, 1861, as the 6th Massachusetts men passed through Baltimore on their way to Washington, D.C., they were attacked by a mob of secessionists, who believed the Southern states had the right to withdraw from the United States and practice self-government. In the fighting that followed, four soldiers and twelve Baltimore citizens were killed.

Angry secessionists in Baltimore tried to block the arrival of more Union troops. They tore up railroad tracks, burned bridges, and destroyed telegraph lines. Scared civilians in Washington, D.C., feared that, if more Union troops did not arrive quickly, the city would be taken over by Confederates. But more Union regiments did arrive, via steamers and alternate train routes. As the news of the violence at Baltimore spread, it only strengthened the resolve of the Union regiments that were waiting to depart.

The United States needed someone to lead its new army of volunteers. Winfield Scott and John Wool, the only two United States generals with any actual battle experience, were both in their seventies. Though they could offer strategic advice, they were too old to withstand the hardships of battle. The most promising eligible officer was a Virginian and West Point graduate named Robert E. Lee, who had distinguished himself in the Mexican War. On April 18, 1861, four days after Fort Sumter's fall, President Lincoln asked Lee if he would take command of the Union Army.

Lee hesitated. He was not a secessionist, but he was loyal to his home state. He decided to wait and see what action Virginia took. One day later, Virginia sided with the South and seceded from the Union. Unable to fight against his fellow Virginians, Lee resigned from the United States Army. Much to Lincoln's dismay, he accepted command of the Confederate Army of Virginia.

Lincoln searched for someone else to lead the Union Army. Later, General Irvin McDowell, one of the men chosen to lead the United States Army, warned President Lincoln that the Union men were inexperienced. "You are green, it is true, but they are green, also," Lincoln said, referring to the Confederate troops. "You are all green alike."[1] Both Union and

President Lincoln first tried to enlist Robert E. Lee, seen here after the end of the war, as the leader of the Union armies. Lee, loyal to his state of Virginia, decided to fight for the Confederacy.

Confederate officers and soldiers were inexperienced. They were unsure of what to expect when they finally went into their first battle.

Battle of Bull Run

Ever since the volunteers had gathered in Washington, D.C., they had been eager to strike back at the Confederacy for its attack on Fort Sumter. Throughout the North, soldiers and civilians alike were eager to see the United States Army march on Richmond, Virginia, the capital of the Confederacy. In July 1861, the North began its trek into the Confederacy. Thirty thousand Union Army volunteers

Patriotism ran high in the North after the attack on Fort Sumter, as Union troops assembled to fight the rebelling Confederate states. President Lincoln is seen here at left, reviewing the Union troops.

left Washington, D.C., and marched southward. During their march, the Union troops sang songs to pass the time. They picked blackberries beside the road during the day and sat around campfires at night. Then the inexperienced United States troops met Confederate troops for the first time near Manassas Junction, Virginia. Nearby was a stream called Bull Run.

The first battle of the Civil War was known as Bull Run in the North and Manassas in the South. The United States military named battles after landmarks, such as rivers or hills. The Confederates, on the other hand, tended to name battles after the town closest to where they took place.

The Battle of Bull Run began with a volley of gun-fire early on Sunday morning, July 21. For the first few hours, the Union Army, dressed in new, mostly blue uniforms and led by General Irvin McDowell, seemed to have the upper hand. As the Union soldiers fought, parties of civilians who had ridden out from Washington to watch the battle could be seen in the distance. Men and women in horse-drawn carriages had brought picnic lunches with them, as if they were going to watch an outdoor concert. Among the spectators were some of the most prominent members of Washington society. They waved handkerchiefs at the Union soldiers.

By late afternoon, however, the Union soldiers were growing tired and thirsty. Meanwhile, the Confederate forces rallied with the arrival of reinforcements. The Confederates advanced and managed to push the Union soldiers backward. Suddenly, the Union men began retreating, running over each other in their attempt to flee the advancing enemy. The spectators, fearful for their lives, began to flee, too. Ladies dropped their parasols and lost their hats as carriages and horses dashed away from the scene of the lost battle. Approximately forty-five hundred men, both Union and Confederate, were killed, wounded, or captured at the Battle of Bull Run.

After their retreat, the scattered Union troops filtered back into Washington. Their regiments were out of order and jumbled together. The loss of Bull Run was an embarrassment to the Union. "We are utterly and disgracefully routed, beaten, whipped by secessionists," wrote George Templeton Strong, a New York lawyer and civic leader.[2]

After Bull Run, the reality that the nation was at war with itself began to sink in to the Union troops. Some of them only now fully realized the gravity of what they had signed up to do. Men had been killed at Bull Run, and all of their lives had been in danger. The Confederates were not sissies, after all. Responding to the disaster at Bull Run, the United States government asked for one hundred thousand new recruits. Already it appeared the existing volunteers would be needed longer than the ninety days for which they had enlisted. The nation was broken. Its two halves were at war.

DIFFERENT WORLDS

The Northern and Southern regions of the United States were two very different worlds at the time of the Civil War. Not only were their populations dramatically different, but their climates, economies, and cultures were vastly different as well.

At the onset of the Civil War, there were 22 million white people and approximately 250,000 free blacks living in the North. By contrast, the Southern states had a much smaller population of 8 million whites, 4.5 million slaves, and 250,000 free blacks.[1] While both regions were predominantly rural, the North was more rapidly becoming urban than the South, which had fewer large cities. The Southern economy was based on agricultural work performed primarily by black slaves. New immigrants, therefore, did not settle in the South as frequently as they did in the North, where there were more job opportunities. Thus, while Southern society retained its traditional mix of elite white planters, slaves, white yeoman farmers, and free blacks, Northern society became more ethnically diverse with its influx of immigrant labor.

Changes in Agriculture

Since the earliest colonial settlements, agriculture had been both a way of life and the basis for the American economy. But agriculture had developed differently in the North and South. In the South, cash-crop plantations grew and marketed a single crop, such as tobacco or cotton. This Southern plantation economy relied on slave labor in order to produce large quantities of raw materials. These raw materials were then exported, mainly to mills in Great Britain. Black slaves did all the work of tending and harvesting crops. White plantation owners depended on the success of the plantation for their living.

In addition to plantations, the South had small farms that were run by poorer whites. Many white farmers who did not have their own land might become sharecroppers—farmers who worked a portion of another person's land in exchange for a share of the profits. The economy of the South in the 1800s was much the same as it had been in the 1700s.

In contrast, the economy in the Northern states changed dramatically during the 1800s. Small individual farms were common in the North. But after 1800, mills and factories devoted to manufacturing began to develop as well. A booming textile industry was beginning to transform the North into a populated area with a stable economic base. By 1860, textile mills employed 115,000 free white Americans.[2] Half of these workers were female or foreign-born. New immigrants seeking jobs flocked to the mills. So did

The South's economy, which consisted of growing cash crops such as cotton for profit, was based on the use of slave labor.

young unmarried women who had left family farms to earn a living of their own. Though most people remained farmers, this new class of wage-earning laborers was growing. The rapid rise of Northern manufacturing contrasted sharply with the lack of change in the Southern economy. The Northern economy was becoming more diversified, while the Southern economy continued to rely on a centuries-old system of plantation agriculture.

A Transportation Revolution

The Northern economy was given another huge boost by new developments in transportation. In 1825, workers completed the 363-mile-long Erie Canal, which linked the Great Lakes to the Atlantic Ocean. Railroads, which began to be built in the United States in 1830, connected different regions. Steamboats, first made commercially in 1807, reduced traveling time between ports.

Goods and people could now travel much faster than ever before. These transportation developments, however, were concentrated in the North. Previously, travel in the American interior had been by sailboat and raft, up and down the major rivers, and then by stagecoach over land. Farmers in the western states had always used the Mississippi River to transport their goods. But now railroads linked the Midwest with the East, and people were no longer as dependent on the rivers for transportation. As a result, the flow of goods began to shift away from the old North-South pattern up and down the major rivers to more of an east-west pattern via railroads and canals, which were concentrated in the North and Midwest.[3] Because goods and passengers could now travel from east to west much faster, the two regions became linked.

By 1860, there were still more people living on farms than in cities in the Northern United States. But rural living had changed considerably. Traditionally, farm families had produced only what was needed for their own households, along with a small surplus. The surplus could be traded with others for goods they could not produce themselves. However, as new transportation developments began to expand the economy, farmers started growing more crops to sell. In 1820, only one third of the food grown in rural areas of the Northeast was intended for market. By 1860, this figure had grown to two thirds.[4] More and more people were becoming involved in trade.

New markets and new trade routes were created by the transportation revolution in the United States. Grain grown in the fertile western plains was now transported to eastern markets. This brought eastern and western farmers into direct competition. Small farmers in the Northeast could not compete with the Midwest farmers. In the Northeast, all the eligible land was already under cultivation. Expansion was impossible. Soil exhaustion from worn-out land resulted in lower crop yields, and the uneven New England terrain did not lend itself to the new farm machinery of the 1850s, such as mechanical sowers, reapers, threshers, and balers. Many New England farmers sold their land and moved to the Midwest, where the land was better for farming. Others took factory jobs in the growing textile mills.

Those who stayed on the farm adapted to the conditions they faced. Rather than attempt to produce corn or wheat commercially, they raised livestock and specialized in dairy farming or fruit and vegetable production. Because meat, fruits, vegetables, and milk could not be kept fresh for long, people who produced these items locally had an advantage over distant competitors, despite better ways to transport goods. Still, the transportation revolution of the 1800s had a significant impact on the economy in the Northern half of the United States.

Rise of American Manufacturing

In the North, all kinds of dramatic changes were taking place in the 1800s. New means of transportation, the rise of commercial farming and manufacturing, a growing population, and an industrial boom all helped change the pace of life in the North. The South, however, lagged behind. Fewer developments in transportation and industrialization took place in the South. The Southern agricultural economy remained much the same as it had been in the previous century, although inventions such as the cotton gin did make plantations more productive. The South remained primarily agricultural, while the North had begun to develop a manufacturing base. Because the South did not produce many manufactured goods, it relied on Europe and the North to supply those items.

By 1850, Northern factories and mills, concentrated in the states of Massachusetts, Connecticut, Rhode Island, New York, Pennsylvania, and Ohio, produced 90 percent of all the manufactured goods made in the United States.[5] This represented a huge change. Before 1800, most manufactured goods, such as cloth, clothing, or shoes, were produced by individual craftsmen in small shops or by women at home. Before the rise of textile mills, women wove fabric at home and itinerant, or roaming, weavers traveled the countryside, making cloth for people. In the early 1800s, factories began to replace home manufacturing. Water-powered mills capable of producing large quantities of fabric were built along New England rivers. By 1860, there were textile mills all over New England. These mills employed tens of thousands of people. Because mills could mass-produce cotton, linen, and other fabrics, the price for these items decreased. Power looms could make cloth so quickly and cheaply that many women stopped weaving their own cloth and began buying machine-made cloth.

This Northern industrial revolution was fueled in part by the development of interchangeable parts. Eli Whitney, the inventor of the cotton gin, helped promote the idea of interchangeable parts—standard, machine-made pieces for equipment.[6] Then another businessman, Samuel Colt, started using interchangeable parts in his firearms business. By mass-producing weapons with interchangeable parts created by precision machinery, Colt could ensure that all his revolvers would be uniform. Previously, guns had been made by hand. It was a time-consuming process that required considerable skill. Each gun would be slightly different, with different-sized parts. Now, an unskilled laborer could take the standardized machine-made parts of a gun and put them together quickly. Because the weapons could be mass-produced, they cost less than handmade ones. Soon many different industries increased their production by using interchangeable parts.

The Reform Movement in the North

As the industrial revolution enlarged the Northern economy, the standard of living for people in the North also rose. More families became financially well-off. A middle class developed, in which men worked outside the home and women were homemakers. Because they enjoyed a higher standard of living than before, this new middle class had more free time.

To put this free time to good use, many middle-class Northerners, both women and men, became involved in reform societies. These societies promoted different causes such as moral living, temperance (non-consumption of alcohol), religion, and abolition (the elimination of slavery). Middle-class Northerners were eager to improve the world around them. A few became active reformers.

Technological changes and an influx of immigrants from Europe caused American society to change rapidly. Thousands of immigrants from places such as Germany and Ireland had altered the ethnic makeup of Northern society. It had become much more diverse. This mix of cultures caused many Anglo-American Northerners to worry. They feared that the customs and cultures of foreign-born citizens would change life in the United States.

Some Americans reacted to these changes they perceived by participating in reform crusades. Reformers formed charities to help and uplift the working poor. Some reformers worked to improve conditions in prisons and mental asylums. Others preached temperance or denounced slavery. The antislavery movement would soon become one of the strongest reform movements in the North.

The Antislavery Movement in the North

Opposition to slavery took many forms. Not all those who opposed slavery believed that blacks were equal to whites or deserved the same rights. Many doubted whether a free black population could be absorbed into the United States. They worried about where blacks would go if they were freed.

One group of antislavery advocates had long proposed a solution to this problem. The American Colonization Society, formed in 1816, believed in resettling freed slaves in Africa. Colonizationists, as supporters of resettlement were called, helped found an African colony called Liberia. Small numbers of freed slaves were resettled there in the 1820s. But most African Americans did not want to be sent to Africa. The majority of blacks wanted to remain in the only country they had ever known. But they also wanted to enjoy the same freedom, rights, and opportunities as white people.

In 1833, the American Anti-Slavery Society, an organization of abolitionists, including New York merchants Arthur and Lewis Tappan and outspoken newspaper publisher William Lloyd Garrison, was formed. The society published antislavery literature, some of which was sent to the South. Sometimes Southern mobs would seize abolitionist publications and destroy them before they could be distributed. Southerners feared that abolitionists would stir up rebellion among their slaves, so they tried to silence antislavery voices. In 1837, Elijah Lovejoy, the editor of an abolitionist newspaper in Illinois, was murdered by a mob of proslavery men.

In 1831, William Lloyd Garrison began publishing his radical abolitionist paper, *The Liberator*, in Boston. Garrison, who was white, soon became known as an extremist for the cause of immediate abolition. He refused to compromise on the issue of slavery and condemned politicians who tried to do so. "I am aware that many object to the severity of my language," he acknowledged, "[but] on this subject I do not wish to think, or speak, or write, with moderation. I am in earnest—I will not equivocate—I will not excuse—I

will not retreat a single inch—and I will be heard."[7]
Protesting Congress's history of compromising over
slavery, Garrison once burned a copy of the
Constitution before a shocked audience. He shouted,
"So perish all compromises with tyranny!"[8]
Abolitionists like Garrison believed in immediate,
uncompensated emancipation. They did not believe
slave owners should be paid, or compensated, for the
loss of their property if their slaves were freed. To
Garrison, slavery was a moral wrong.

John Brown was another radical abolitionist. He
believed in freeing the slaves through any means necessary. He often helped runaway slaves escape to the
North and to Canada, where slavery was illegal. In
1859, John Brown tried to start a slave rebellion in
Harpers Ferry, Virginia (now West Virginia). The
rebellion failed, and Brown was captured and hanged
for treason. But Brown's death, in the eyes of some
Northern foes of slavery, made him a martyr for the
cause of abolition.

Not all abolitionists were as militant as Garrison
and Brown. Others, such as Arthur and Lewis Tappan,
were content to stay in the background, donating their
money and time to the American Anti-Slavery Society.
Women were also involved in the abolition movement.
Sisters Angelina and Sarah Grimké, who hailed from
South Carolina, toured the North and lectured against
slavery.

In 1851, Harriet Beecher Stowe accomplished
more for the antislavery cause than any abolitionist

John Brown, a militant abolitionist, became a martyr to the cause of freedom for the slaves when he was executed for leading a failed slave revolt in Virginia.

newspaper or speaker ever had. Stowe wrote a novel called *Uncle Tom's Cabin*, which described life on a slave plantation. Though Southerners charged that Stowe's account was inaccurate, Northerners could not get enough of the book. It sold more than three hundred thousand copies in just one year. Readers sympathized with the slave characters and wept when one of them was sold by his master and separated from his wife and children. *Uncle Tom's Cabin* raised so much antislavery sentiment in the North that President Abraham Lincoln is later said to have referred to Stowe as "the little lady that started this great war [the Civil War]."[9]

SOURCE DOCUMENT

MY DEAR MRS. STOWE—

I SAT UP LAST NIGHT UNTIL LONG AFTER ONE O'CLOCK, READING AND FINISHING "UNCLE TOM'S CABIN." I COULD NOT LEAVE IT ANY MORE THAN I COULD HAVE LEFT A DYING CHILD; NOR COULD I RESTRAIN AN ALMOST HYSTERICAL SOBBING FOR AN HOUR AFTER I LAID MY HEAD UPON MY PILLOW. I THOUGHT I WAS A THOROUGHGOING ABOLITIONIST BEFORE, BUT YOUR BOOK HAS AWAKENED SO STRONG A FEELING OF INDIGNATION AND OF COMPASSION, THAT I SEEM NEVER TO HAVE HAD ANY FEELING ON THIS SUBJECT TILL NOW.[10]

Uncle Tom's Cabin *moved many people to want to fight for the freedom of the slaves. This letter, written by an unknown woman, showed the impact Stowe's book made on some people.*

The antislavery movement angered and worried Southerners, who saw it as a threat to their way of life. Slave owners resented the North's condemnation of slavery. They argued that Northern factories and mills practiced a form of "wage slavery" by employing white workers at very low wages. Some Southerners said that Northern wage slavery was more inhumane than Southern slavery. They argued that factory owners paid workers low wages and then fired them when they became sick or old. In contrast, some slave owners (though by no means all) cared for their slaves when they became unable to work, treating them as relatives rather than as employees.

Among the strongest supporters of the antislavery movement were free blacks and escaped slaves such as Sojourner Truth, Frederick Douglass, and Harriet Tubman, who worked hard to help slaves attain their freedom. There were approximately half a million free blacks living in the United States before the Civil War. Half of them lived in the North, mainly in cities such as New York, Philadelphia, Cincinnati, and Baltimore. As early as 1830, the free black population in the United States had started more than fifty anti-slavery societies.

Life of Free Blacks in the North

Most Northern states had begun to abolish slavery even before 1800. Opportunities for free blacks were often far better in the North than in the South. Still, free blacks in the North did not always have the same

Frederick Douglass was one of the best known leaders of the abolition movement.

legal rights and privileges as white citizens. Some states passed laws that required free blacks to pay a bond of $500 to $1,000 to ensure their good behavior. Before the Civil War, only the states of Massachusetts, Rhode Island, New Hampshire, Maine, and Vermont allowed blacks the same voting rights as whites. Only Massachusetts allowed blacks on juries. Blacks were often barred from public facilities in the North. When abolitionist Frederick Douglass traveled through the North on a speaking tour in 1844, he often found himself barred from hotels, restaurants, and theaters because of his race. Despite the widespread antislavery movement, many, if not most, Northerners did not want to be equal to blacks. In fact, many Northerners opposed slavery not for moral reasons, but because they feared it would spread and ruin the balance of slave states and free states in Congress.

To improve their lives, Northern free blacks formed their own organizations. They organized mutual-aid societies, which helped them get jobs and insurance. Free blacks formed their own churches, newspapers, fraternal societies, schools, and antislavery organizations. Black abolitionist societies helped fugitive slaves and publicly condemned slavery.

Recognizing that education was one way to improve their situation, free blacks started their own private schools. In 1820, Sarah Mapps Douglas, a member of a well-to-do family of free blacks in Philadelphia, opened a private school for black children that became one of ten such schools in Philadelphia. Later, she worked at the Institute for Colored Youth, a black-run institution for higher education. Schools for free blacks flourished in areas with large African-American populations, but they did not fare as well elsewhere.

While technically free, blacks were not always welcomed into Northern society. In 1833, Prudence Crandall, a white woman living in Canterbury, Connecticut, began to admit free black girls into her school for young ladies. Immediately, she faced opposition from local townspeople who withdrew their own daughters from the school. Undaunted, Crandall reopened her school as an institution for black girls only, but she lost the patronage of local citizens and was harassed by townspeople who feared an influx of free blacks into their community. Townspeople threw manure in her well, merchants refused to sell goods to her, and her school was set on fire and its windows were broken. Several years later, Crandall closed the school and moved away.

As the antislavery movement gained strength, more people in the North began to question whether slavery should be allowed to exist. Many did not want to see slavery continue. This raised another important question: Who would decide the fate of slavery, the individual states or the federal (national) government?

States' Rights Versus Federal Authority

Since the founding of the United States, American politicians had argued over who should have ultimate power, the states or the federal government. One of the most famous and well-documented of these arguments was the Webster-Hayne debate of 1830. For two days, Senator Daniel Webster of Massachusetts and Senator Robert Hayne of South Carolina debated on the floor of the Senate. The balcony of the Senate overflowed with people who crowded in to hear the men speak.

Webster and Hayne's debate focused on the doctrine of nullification—the theory that the individual states had the power to veto federal legislation that conflicted with their own laws. Hayne believed in nullification. Unless the states had the ability to nullify oppressive laws, Hayne argued, they would always be subject to the tyranny of the federal government. Webster disagreed. He feared what would happen if the states did not give up any of their authority to the federal government. The outcome, he said, would be "states dissevered, discordant, belligerent; on a land rent with civil feuds, or drenched . . . in fraternal blood!"[11] Webster argued that, if nullification were allowed, it would leave the federal government powerless. We must not have "Liberty first and Union afterwards," he insisted, "but . . . Liberty *and* Union, now and for ever, one and inseparable."[12]

The idea of nullification had long been promoted by United States Vice President John C. Calhoun, a South Carolinian, who was a strong supporter of states' rights. At a state convention in 1832, South Carolina refused to accept a protective tariff passed by the federal government. This tariff would have placed higher taxes on imported goods such as wool and iron. South Carolina used the doctrine of nullification to justify its refusal to accept the tariff.

United States President Andrew Jackson did not want a conflict between the state and federal governments, but he was determined to uphold the authority of the federal government. Jackson got authority from Congress to send troops to South Carolina to enforce the tariff. The disagreement over the tariff reflected the larger debate on the question of states' rights versus federal authority. This question had never been resolved. When citizens began to argue over whether slavery should be allowed to spread into the Western territories of the United States, the question of who had more power—and who would decide whether slavery would continue and be allowed to expand to the West—became even more important.

A NATION DIVIDED

From its beginning, the United States wrestled with the issue of slavery. To avoid confrontation, Congress had always compromised on the issue. When framing the Constitution in 1787, the Founding Fathers could not agree on how to handle the issue of slavery and representation in Congress. So they compromised—each slave would count as three fifths of a person for purposes of representation.

In 1820, another compromise was made over slavery when the Missouri Territory petitioned the Union for admission as a slave state. At that time, there was a balance of eleven free and eleven slave states in the Union. If Missouri were admitted as a slave state, it would tilt the political balance in favor of the slave states. Because Missouri lay next to several free states, its admission as a slave state would also move slavery farther north. Though Southerners were eager to secure more slave territory, many Northerners did not want to see the power and influence of the South spread. As a result, they opposed the expansion of slavery into the territories. To resolve the issue, Congress worked out an agreement known as the Missouri

Compromise. Under its terms, Missouri was admitted to the Union as a slave state. However, another free state, Maine, which had been carved out of Massachusetts, was admitted at the same time, keeping the balance of slave and free states equal. In addition, Congress outlawed slavery in the Louisiana Territory north of the 36th parallel of latitude (the southern boundary of Missouri).

Aging former President Thomas Jefferson foresaw problems with the Missouri Compromise. He feared that the compromise only masked deep regional divisions between the North and South that would not go away and that might one day lead to great conflict. Former President John Quincy Adams also realized that the slavery question could not be compromised forever. "I take it for granted," Adams said, "that the present question is a mere preamble—a title page to a great tragic volume."[1] Both former presidents were keenly aware that different ideas about states' rights, slavery, and the Union would one day bring the nation into conflict.

The Wilmot Proviso

Whether slavery should be allowed to spread into new territory became a burning issue in American politics in the mid-nineteenth century. Though it was unclear if the land in the new territories was suitable for plantation agriculture, Southerners wanted to preserve their right to take slaves there. When the United States won land from Mexico after the Mexican War in 1846, a Pennsylvanian congressman named David Wilmot suggested that slavery be prohibited in these new territories. His idea, which became known as the Wilmot Proviso, did not pass. However, it started a national debate on whether slavery should be allowed to spread into new territories.

Many Northerners, even those who were not abolitionists, still feared the growth of slave power. They wanted the new western territories to become home to free white settlers, not slave owners and their plantations. Thus, although they were not morally opposed to slavery, many whites did not want to see it spread to areas where it might jeopardize the livelihood of free white settlers. People who felt this way were called Free-Soilers. Abolitionists, those who were morally opposed to slavery, also opposed the spread of slavery into new territory. Abolitionists were outnumbered by Free-Soilers in the North, but both groups agreed that slavery should at least be limited to the areas where it already existed.

The Compromise of 1850

When California settlers petitioned the United States government for admission as a free state in 1850, they provoked yet another compromise over slavery. Slave-owning Southerners, eager to open more territory to slavery, did not want California or any of the lands gained from Mexico to become free states. They argued that at least the lower half of California, that part below the 36th parallel, ought to be open to

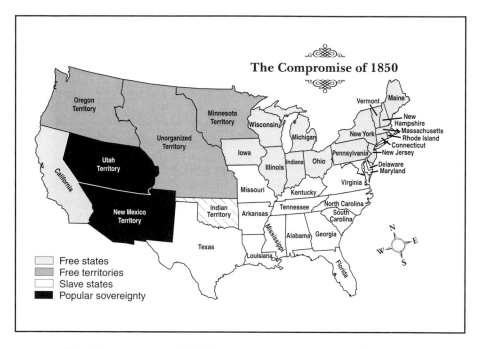

The Compromise of 1850 was an attempt to save the Union by addressing the tension between the Northern free states and the slaveholding states of the South.

slavery. Those who had settled in California, however, wanted it to be a free state.

Under the Compromise of 1850, developed in part by Kentucky Senator Henry Clay, who had also helped create the Missouri Compromise, California was admitted to the Union as a free state. However, the rest of the territories gained from Mexico were left open to popular sovereignty. That is, the settlers who moved there would vote to decide whether the areas would become free states or slave states. In addition, Congress passed a stronger fugitive slave law designed to help return runaway slaves to their owners. Under this law, anyone who found a runaway slave was supposed to turn the suspect over to the police. No evidence was required to prove that a person was really an escaped slave, and the suspects were not allowed a trial by jury. Federal authorities were also given financial incentives to round up fugitives.

Opposition to the Fugitive Slave Law

Abolitionists despised the new fugitive slave law because it required them to help slave owners recover their property. Many vowed to disobey the law, claiming that their duty was to a higher, moral law. Besides, they argued, it was unconstitutional to hand a person over to the police on the mere suspicion that he or she might be a runaway slave. Abolitionists argued that all suspects should be given legal counsel and that they should be proven guilty in court before being sent south.

Southerners were angered by the lack of Northern support for the Fugitive Slave Law. Not wanting to lose Southern customers, many prominent New York businessmen signed a letter of support for the law. The merchants who refused to support the law were blacklisted in the South, and the names of their companies were printed in Southern newspapers. The newspapers encouraged their readers to boycott, or refuse to buy goods from, these companies on the grounds that their owners were "agitators" or "abolitionists." One of the blacklisted companies was Bowen McNamee and Co., a silk and dry goods firm run in part by Henry

Chandler Bowen, the son-in-law of abolitionist Lewis Tappan. Bowen, who also published an abolitionist newspaper called *The Independent*, was no fan of the Fugitive Slave Law. Facing a boycott of his business, Bowen boldly circulated flyers informing the public that it was his goods, and not his principles, that were for sale. "The attempt to punish us as merchants for the exercise of our liberty as citizens we leave to the judgement of the community," Bowen wrote in 1850.[2]

Because the Fugitive Slave Law tried to force people to help return runaway slaves, it caused widespread anger in the North. Abolitionists and others asked themselves whether they, too, had become slaves to the South. Northern Free-Soilers, who wanted the western territories to be open to free white people only, formed a political party. Called the Free-Soil party, it was dedicated to stopping the spread of slavery into the territories.

Kansas-Nebraska Act

Growing tensions between pro- and antislavery forces were made worse by the passage of the Kansas-Nebraska Act in 1854. The law upset the boundaries for free and slave states set by the old Missouri Compromise. Proposed by Senator Stephen Douglas of Illinois, the Kansas-Nebraska Act left the fate of the Kansas and Nebraska territories up to popular sovereignty, or the vote of the people who settled there. Under the terms of the old Missouri Compromise, all land north of the 36th parallel had been closed off to slavery. Since the entire Kansas-Nebraska territory was north of this line, it would have been closed to slavery under the Missouri Compromise. However, with the passage of the Kansas-Nebraska Act and the theory of popular sovereignty, it was now available as slave territory if settlers there wished it to be. Though the Kansas-Nebraska bill was fiercely opposed by abolitionists and Free-Soilers, it managed to pass through Congress and become law in 1854. After its passage, people in the North began to worry that proslavery interests posed a threat to their free way of life.

Bleeding Kansas

Under the doctrine of popular sovereignty, whoever settled in Kansas and Nebraska would get to decide whether Kansas and Nebraska became free states or slave states. As a result, both pro- and antislavery forces rushed to settle the territory with their supporters. Nebraska was settled mostly by antislavery Northerners. Kansas, on the other hand, became the center of a tug-of-war between proslavery and antislavery interests. Abolitionists raised money to send Free-Soilers to Kansas, and armed them with rifles to protect their point of view. Proslavery Southerners also sent people to stake claims in the territory and improve its chances of becoming a slave state.

When elections were held in the Kansas Territory in 1855, thousands of proslavery Missourians crossed the border and posed as settlers in order to vote illegally in the election. Convinced the election was corrupt, Free-Soilers refused to acknowledge the new proslavery legislature and set up their own government. Soon, the different settlers were battling over the future of the territory. Abolitionist John Brown, who later become famous for his attempt to start a slave rebellion in Harpers Ferry, Virginia, teamed up with a group of abolitionist settlers and murdered five proslavery settlers in Kansas. Frequent violence between slavery and antislavery forces soon earned the territory the nickname "Bleeding Kansas."

Tensions between pro- and antislavery forces even spilled over into the chambers of Congress. In 1856, after speaking out against the spread of slavery into Kansas and denouncing Senator Andrew P. Butler of South Carolina, Massachusetts Senator Charles Sumner, a vocal antislavery advocate, was attacked by Congressman Preston Brooks of South Carolina. Brooks, who was Senator Butler's nephew, approached Sumner's desk on the floor of the Senate and beat Sumner over the head with a cane until he became unconscious. Sumner received massive head injuries and never fully recovered from the beating. The incident polarized public opinion. Sumner's supporters accused Brooks of trying to suppress free speech in the Senate, while Southerners applauded Brooks's action, sending him new canes in a show of support. Even the nation's elected officials could not agree to disagree over the issue of slavery.

Dred Scott

While violence over the slavery issue spread, a black slave from Missouri was making judicial history. In 1857, a slave named Dred Scott sued his master for his freedom. Scott had been the property of an army surgeon who took him to the free state of Illinois for several years and then to the Wisconsin Territory, where, under the terms of the Missouri Compromise, slavery was not allowed. Scott argued that, because he had lived in free areas for so many years, he ought to be free.

His case passed from court to court, eventually making its way to the United States Supreme Court. In a controversial ruling, the Supreme Court, which was composed of five Southerners and four Northerners, decided to overturn the Missouri Compromise. They rejected the notion that Congress had the right to ban slavery in the territories. Therefore, the fact that he had lived in free territory did not make him a free man. Furthermore, they argued, Dred Scott, as a black man, was not a citizen of the United States.

The *Dred Scott* decision was received like a bombshell by antislavery people in the North. Abolitionists were appalled by the Court's decision that Congress did not have the right to bar slavery. Free-Soilers were also angry. They feared slavery would now spread to areas that had been free.

An ambitious lawyer from Illinois named Abraham Lincoln was able to sum up Northern fears over the

SOURCE DOCUMENT

THE [FRAMERS OF THE CONSTITUTION] PERFECTLY UNDERSTOOD THE MEANING OF THE LANGUAGE THEY USED AND HOW IT WOULD BE UNDERSTOOD BY OTHERS; AND THEY KNEW THAT IT WOULD NOT IN ANY PART OF THE CIVILIZED WORLD BE SUPPOSED TO EMBRACE THE NEGRO RACE, WHICH, BY COMMON CONSENT, HAD BEEN EXCLUDED FROM CIVILIZED GOVERNMENTS AND THE FAMILY OF NATIONS AND DOOMED TO SLAVERY. . . . THE UNHAPPY BLACK RACE WERE SEPARATED FROM THE WHITE . . . AND WERE NEVER THOUGHT OF OR SPOKEN OF EXCEPT AS PROPERTY AND WHEN THE CLAIMS OF THE OWNER OR THE PROFIT OF THE TRADER WERE SUPPOSED TO NEED PROTECTION.[3]

The Dred Scott *decision, which insisted that no black person could be a citizen of the United States, infuriated Northerners. It made Southerners happy because it argued that Congress had no right to limit the expansion of slavery into new territories.*

spread of slavery. "'A house divided against itself cannot stand,'" Lincoln reasoned in 1858.

I believe this government cannot endure permanently, half slave and half free. I do not expect the Union to be dissolved—I do not expect the House to fall—but I do expect it to cease to be divided. It will become all one thing, or all the other. Either the opponents of slavery will arrest the further spread of it, and place it where the public mind shall rest in the belief that it is in the course of ultimate extinction; or its advocates will push it forward, till it shall become alike lawful in all the States, old as well as new, North as well as South.[4]

The Splintering of the Political Parties

In the 1850s, the two major national political parties, the Democrats and the Whigs, were torn apart by the issue of slavery. People began changing their political affiliation to align themselves on one side or the other of the slavery issue. For example, with antislavery sentiment growing in the North, many Northern Democrats were no longer willing to support the proslavery views of Southern Democrats. People changed parties in order to express their beliefs.

Political realignments like these caused the traditional Democratic and Whig parties to fall apart. Neither party had a national audience anymore. Instead, they began to rely on regional support. Smaller political parties soon sprang up, based on a single theme. Among them were the Know-Nothing, or Nativist, party, which opposed the influx of immigrants, and the Free-Soil party, which opposed the spread of slavery to the western territories. After the passage of the Kansas-Nebraska Act, the Whig party separated into Northern and Southern wings. Then it fell apart completely.

The collapse of the Whigs led to the formation of a new political party, called the Republican party, which emerged after the Kansas-Nebraska Act in 1854. The Republican party, which nearly won the presidential election in 1856, was supported only by Northerners. Among those who joined the Republican party were antislavery Whigs and Democrats, abolitionists, Free-Soilers, and Know-Nothings.

The Election of 1860 and Secession

The year 1860 brought an unusual election. The United States was divided over the issues of slavery and states' rights, and the political parties ran four different candidates for the presidency. The Republicans nominated Abraham Lincoln from Springfield, Illinois, who opposed the spread of slavery. The Democrats, unable to find one candidate who could satisfy everyone, ran two candidates: Stephen Douglas of Illinois for the Northern Democrats, and John Breckinridge of Kentucky for the Southern Democrats. The new Constitutional Union party, which took no stand on slavery and was simply committed to the preservation of the Union, ran John Bell from Tennessee. Abraham Lincoln, who was not even on the ballot in some Southern states, won the election held in November.

Protesting the election of a president who was opposed to the spread of slavery, South Carolina seceded from the Union in December 1860. Many Southerners refused to acknowledge Lincoln's election. One Virginia newspaper went so far as to call Lincoln's election "the greatest evil that has ever befallen this country."[5] Soon, Alabama, Florida, Georgia, Louisiana, Mississippi, and Texas also withdrew from the Union. In February 1861, these states joined to form the Confederate States of America. They chose a slave owner and former United States senator named Jefferson Davis to be their president.

Abraham Lincoln's election to the presidency so enraged Southerners that several states began preparations to leave the Union.

President-elect Lincoln faced the enormous task of uniting a nation that was rapidly falling apart. After his election, he received multiple death threats from secessionists who hated him because he opposed the extension of slavery into the territories. Lincoln's advisors even feared he might be assassinated on his way from Illinois to Washington, so they made him get off the heavily decorated presidential train in Philadelphia. While the presidential train went on without him, acting as a decoy, Lincoln secretly boarded another train that took him quietly to Washington. Elected at a time when the country was experiencing its greatest turmoil, Lincoln became the only president-elect ever to have to sneak into the nation's capital.

In his inaugural speech on March 4, 1861, President Lincoln reminded the seceding states that the government had no desire to engage in civil war. "You can have no conflict, without being yourselves the aggressors," he said. Determined to reunite a broken Union, Lincoln then reached out to the departed states, telling them, "though passion may have strained it must not break our bonds of affection."[6]

The Attack on Fort Sumter

The bonds of affection were broken a month later, on April 12, 1861, when Confederate forces fired on federal soldiers at Fort Sumter in Charleston Harbor, South Carolina. Since Christmas of 1860, South Carolina militiamen had surrounded the federal garrison of Fort Sumter, preventing the troops inside from receiving any supplies. The troops inside Sumter, led by Major Robert Anderson of Kentucky, were now running out of food. Lincoln had long wanted to send them provisions, but he did not want to risk starting a war. Finally, after months of waiting, he decided the nation had to act.

Lincoln informed the governor of South Carolina that he was planning to send supplies to the federal troops. Hoping to avoid conflict, however, he assured the governor that he would not send any weapons or reinforcements, so long as the Confederates did not attack the fort. Immediately, the Confederates sent

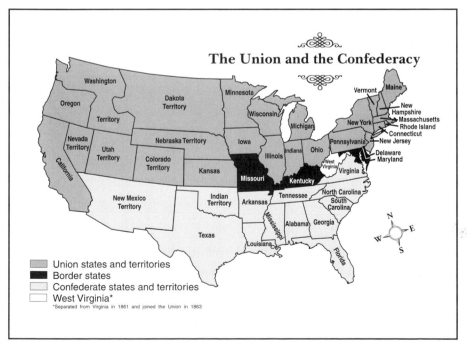

Ultimately, all of the states would be divided in loyalty to either the Union or the Confederacy.

messengers to Major Anderson, who told him to surrender or face attack. Major Anderson refused to surrender. As a result, the Confederates attacked Fort Sumter in the early morning of April 12, 1861. The attack marked the beginning of the Civil War.

After the attack on Fort Sumter, Virginia decided to join the Confederacy. Soon, other states of the Upper South followed Virginia in seceding from the Union, until the nation was polarized into two sections. Former countrymen were now enemies. The country's war with itself had begun.

Since leaving home I have not slept in a bed, have not slept once with pantaloons and coat off, have eaten only once at a family table, have not dreamed one dream, have not been homesick, but have wished the war would soon close so that I might join with friends and follow the employment I love. . . .

LIFE IN THE UNION ARMY

—Twenty-three-year-old school-teacher-turned-soldier Private Solomon Stocker of the 30th Ohio Volunteer Infantry.[1]

Like many other volunteers, Solomon Stocker left his sweetheart behind to join the war, and he wrote to her nearly every day. From letters and diaries written by soldiers, and war records kept by the government, we know something of what life was like for a Union soldier.

People Who Served the Union

The average Union soldier was about twenty-five years old.[2] Some, however, such as fourteen-year-old Thomas Lake of the 18th Connecticut regiment, were just boys who left home and headed for the front lines. Even though Thomas Lake was under the required age of eighteen, he and many other underage boys were allowed to join a regiment.

A Union regiment often consisted of many young men, some too young to fight, who were caught up in the excitement of the war.

Every regiment had a color guard or standard bearer who held the regimental battle flag. Some regiments were composed of foot soldiers, or infantry, and others were made up of cavalry or artillery men whose job was to handle and set up the batteries of large cannons used on the battlefield. High-ranking officers usually rode on horseback, as did the cavalry soldiers, who were often sent out on scouting missions.

Some Union regiments had distinctive uniforms. Others wore the standard blue Union Army uniforms. Since regiments were often recruited from a single city or neighborhood, many of the men in a regiment had known one another before the war. Some regiments were composed entirely of one ethnic group, such as Germans or Irish. Among the many other ethnic groups represented in the Union Army were the English, Welsh, Scottish, Canadians, Scandinavians,

French, Swiss, Polish, Italians, Mexicans, and Americans Indians.[3] All together, recent immigrants accounted for about one fourth of the Union Army.[4] In addition, many African Americans fought in the Union Army, although they were not officially recruited until 1863.

The Union Army was made up of many different people playing diverse roles. In addition to soldiers, there were a number of people in the army whose primary role did not involve fighting. These included cooks, officers' servants, surgeons, nurses, hospital crews, quartermasters, and teamsters, or wagon drivers, who had the job of moving supplies via wagon train to wherever the army was encamped. Army engineers were responsible for erecting and destroying bridges and earthworks. Members of the medical corps, along with the three thousand women nurses in the Union Army, cared for the wounded.

The Union Army attracted many additional individuals wherever it camped. Sutlers—businesspeople or storekeepers who sold everything from pastries to oysters—set up shop within army camps and sometimes traveled with the army when it marched. Women seeking extra money offered to wash the soldiers' laundry for them. Photographers also followed the soldiers from camp to camp, documenting the war. They were kept busy taking photographs of soldiers who wanted to send a picture of themselves in uniform to family and friends back home. The most famous of the Civil War photographers was Mathew Brady, who left his portrait business in Washington, D.C., to document the war. Thousands of soldiers had their picture taken by Brady and his assistants.

Life of a Union Soldier

For many Union soldiers, service in the armed forces was an opportunity to see parts of the United States they might otherwise never have seen. Many soldiers had never been away from home and never been to the Southern part of the country. For them, it was like a different world. When Union forces came ashore along the South Carolina coastline, they found plantations abandoned by owners who had fled from the Union invaders. One soldier who had the opportunity to see a plantation off the coast of South Carolina wrote a description home to his parents in New England:

> We found . . . a plantation, and a beautiful one it was. The negro cabins look like cottages and was as neat as most of the houses at home. The master's house was situated in a large garden and was a splendid thing. The sitting room was papered with fresco paper. Most of the furniture had been removed. There was a piano in the room, but it was sadly disfigured and broken. The garden was the handsomest of all. . . . I never saw a garden in New England that looked half so beautiful. We did not see a single person; everything looked as though it had been deserted for some time. I picked a bouquet in the garden that would have brought quite a sum of money at this time of the year in Boston or New York.[5]

The Grand Army of the Republic

Throughout the fall and winter of 1861, part of the Union Army was concentrated in Virginia, where it drilled and trained under the command of General George McClellan. The volunteers eventually became bored with the training exercises. Some began to find out that soldiering was not as exciting as they had imagined it would be. "We have always to be prepared," wrote one soldier during the winter of 1861.

> We have to get up at roll call in the morning (daylight). After roll call we have to pack our blankets in our knapsacks ready for a march at a minute's warning. We then go to breakfast. After breakfast we get ready for dress parade. After that we drill until ten. At half past ten we go on to battalion drill which ends at twelve. After dinner we have to clean our muskets (if they need it) until three, when those who have to go on guard go on guard. Mounting after that, the rest of the company drill an hour. When our day's work is ended, after supper, we do what we please until quarter to nine when drum beats for roll call. After roll call comes taps when we all have to be in bed with lights blowed out. Thus ends the day. This comprises a soldier's life.[6]

After months of routine drill and training exercises, General McClellan managed to turn the Union Army's unschooled soldiers into handsome units that moved together in coordinated motions. McClellan enjoyed training soldiers, and he was well liked among the men. He was reluctant, however, to lead his army into battle. President Lincoln, his advisors, the Union soldiers, and much of the general public were all eager to strike a blow against the South. Especially after the upsetting loss at the Battle of Bull Run, McClellan insisted that his men were not yet ready. Northern officials began to worry that McClellan was stalling. Meanwhile, the cost of feeding, clothing, and supplying the Grand Army of the Republic was growing every day, whether the army did anything or not. By the end of 1862, the Union Army was costing the United States $2.5 million each day.[7]

A Plan to Defeat the South

President Lincoln and his military advisors realized that the North needed to attack the Confederacy on

Boredom could often be intense for Union soldiers as they waited for weeks or months to be sent into battle.

more than one front if it were going to win the war. General Winfield Scott came up with the "anaconda" plan to squeeze the South like a snake. By blockading Confederate ports and sending Union gunboats down the Mississippi, Scott hoped to cut the Confederacy off from all supplies and force it to surrender.

Northern strategy also involved invading the South in a divide-and-conquer tactic. Lincoln selected General Ulysses S. Grant, a West Point graduate from Illinois, to invade the Confederacy from the West, while General George McClellan would attack from the East. Great strides were made on the western front in February 1862 when General Grant's army captured two strategic Confederate outposts in Tennessee. This victory opened up a route into Confederate territory farther south. Grant's next plan was to invade Mississippi, but while he was waiting for reinforcements to join him in Tennessee, Confederate General Albert Sidney Johnston, also a West Point graduate, launched a surprise attack on his army. Johnston's cavalry scouts had discovered the location of the Union Army's camps in Tennessee and had sent word back to their commander, who ordered an attack. The battle between Confederates and Union soldiers that followed took place near a little church named Shiloh, which means "place of peace" in Hebrew. A peach orchard, its trees in full bloom, stood nearby. It was a strange place for so much conflict and tragedy to occur.

General George B. McClellan was President Lincoln's choice to lead the Union armies in the East at the start of the Civil War.

Shiloh

On the morning of April 6, 1862, Albert Sidney Johnston's forces attacked Grant's army, catching it off guard. The surprised Union regiments did their best to muster quickly and fight back. Regiments and companies were separated in the confusion, making it difficult for the Union officers to give commands. The federal artillery men lined up their guns, creating a battery on a nearby hill. They loaded the guns, then fired into the Confederate ranks. Confederate artillery did the same from their position. On both sides, snipers trained their rifles on the enemy.

Union and Confederate infantry, or foot soldiers, were armed with muskets or rifles and sometimes swords, daggers, and revolvers. They swarmed the different arenas of battle, trying to stay with their companies, take aim at the enemy, and avoid injury. The severely wounded lay where they fell, but the injured who could still walk were ordered to the rear of the fight. Some of the horses that carried the cavalry officers were shot, and collapsed beneath their riders. The fighting at Shiloh left a path of destruction wherever it spread: A cornfield was mown flat by gunfire, saplings were snapped in two, and branches and blossoms were blown off trees in the peach orchard.

At first, it looked as though the Union Army were going to lose the fight. Then Confederate General Albert Sidney Johnston was wounded during a fight in the peach orchard. By afternoon, the Confederate commander was dead. When the fighting subsided that evening, there were thousands of wounded men lying next to the silent dead in the fields surrounding Shiloh Church. The injured cried for help or water, but no one dared help them for fear of being attacked by the other side. Both armies were new to battle, and neither side had yet developed a system for collecting their wounded and dead from the field.

On both sides, the soldiers tried to rest and stay dry during the pouring rain that fell that night. When the fighting continued the next day, the Confederates seemed to have lost focus. The Union Army, reinforced by the arrival of more troops, forced the Confederates back to the Mississippi border. Yet it was not a triumphant victory for the Union. Both sides had suffered heavy losses. The Union Army sustained thirteen thousand casualties (dead, wounded, or missing) among its sixty-three thousand men. The Confederates' total casualties were eleven thousand out of forty thousand men, including their fallen leader. Shiloh was the bloodiest battle of the Civil War thus far. It was a devastating loss of human life, far worse than anything Americans at that time had ever known.

The Union Navy

While the Union Army was pursuing its divide-and-conquer strategy, the Union Navy did its best to cripple the Confederacy from the seas. The Civil War ushered in a new era for the United States Navy, and ironclad vessels were the latest in naval technology at the time.

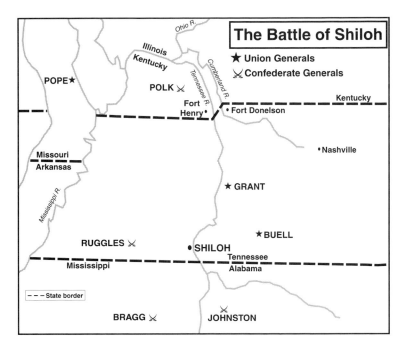

The Battle of Shiloh, one of the bloodiest of the entire war,
began when Confederate General Johnston surprised Union
General Grant's troops.

The Confederacy had a ship called the *Merrimack*,
which had been seized from the North. The
Confederates made it into an ironclad by covering it
with iron plates that acted like armor and were capable
of repelling cannon shot. Ordinary wooden ships were
helpless against an ironclad, and the *Merrimack* was
able to sink the Union ship *Cumberland*.

To challenge the *Merrimack*, the Union Navy com-
missioned a strange-looking ironclad called the
Monitor. The *Monitor* arrived off the coast of Virginia
in March 1862, just in time to fight the *Merrimack*.
The two iron ships clashed and collided, neither

getting the upper hand, until finally the *Merrimack* retreated.

Ironclads were not the only new development in naval technology tried out during the Civil War. The Confederacy had built a hand-cranked submarine called the *Hunley*. In 1864, the *Hunley* became the first submarine ever to sink a ship when it destroyed the Union's *Housatonic* in Charleston Harbor. Unfortunately for the Confederates, the explosion also blew up the *Hunley*, killing its nine-man crew. By trial and error,

The crew of the Union ironclad ship Monitor *(seen here) was sent to try to defeat the Confederate ship* Merrimack *in the first big naval battle of the Civil War.*

both sides developed their knowledge of naval warfare during the Civil War.

Blockade of the South

Hoping to cut off supplies to the Confederacy and force an early end to the war, Union Navy vessels concentrated on blockading, or sealing off, Southern ports. Because the Union Navy did not have enough ships to patrol all the South's coastline at once, some wily ship captains, called blockade runners, managed to sneak past the blockades and bring supplies to Confederate troops and civilians. In addition to its blockade of the Confederacy's eastern ports, the Union Navy concentrated on gaining control of the Mississippi River. From the Mississippi, Union forces could sail down to New Orleans, the largest city in the Confederacy.

In April 1862, after Union gunboats had taken control of the Mississippi River as far south as Memphis, Tennessee, naval officer David G. Farragut led a fleet of twenty-four Union ships on a daring run downriver. Two heavily armed Confederate forts, facing each other on opposite sides of the Mississippi, lay in his path. Both forts were stocked with explosives and cannons, and the river between them had been barricaded with log booms and small boats designed to trap the Union ships in the line of fire. Undaunted by these obstacles, Farragut decided to smash his fleet past the barricades at night. In the predawn hours, Farragut's plan was discovered. The Confederate forts began firing

*David Farragut led the Union naval forces that succeeded
in taking control of the Mississippi River and New Orleans.*

on the Union fleet. Artillery lit up the sky, and Farragut's ships were battered, but twenty of them managed to get past the barricade. When Farragut's fleet reached New Orleans, the surprised Confederate city surrendered to the Union.

Occupying Secessionist Cities

Thanks to its navy, the Union now occupied New Orleans. To control the city, President Lincoln appointed General Benjamin Butler to keep the peace and prevent uprisings. The people of New Orleans resented Butler and the Union presence in their city. Southern women harassed Butler's soldiers in the streets. Some even emptied chamber pots out the window at them. Scenes like these took place in every Southern city that fell to the Union.

In St. Augustine, Florida, which Union soldiers controlled by the summer of 1862, citizens resented the "invaders." "I had quite an adventure a few evenings ago," Stephen J. Wentworth of the 4th New Hampshire Volunteers wrote to his parents:

> I was patrolling the city . . . when I saw a small secession flag waving in one of the windows of one of the largest houses in the city . . . I knocked at the door. . . . I then went up the stairs and into the room . . . where the flag was, and seized it. . . . One of [the women] rushed up and seized hold of the other end of it. . . . She said, You mean miserable Yankee, what do you mean by coming into my house and insulting me? To which I replied, What do you mean by hanging a secession flag in a window under our very face and eyes?[8]

African Americans and the Union Army

While Southerners resented the presence of Union soldiers in their cities, many African-American slaves welcomed the Northern invaders, whom they hoped would set them free. In secessionist cities occupied by the Union, many former slaves volunteered their services to the Union Army. Although blacks had initially been barred from serving in the Union Army, by the summer of 1862, Union Army officers in South Carolina were allowing blacks into their ranks.

During the Civil War, 179,000 black soldiers, many of them former slaves, served in the Union Army. Another 20,000 black sailors served in the Union Navy.[9] There were 166 black regiments, including the famous 54th Massachusetts, led by Colonel Robert Gould Shaw.

Despite their service to the United States, black soldiers were still the victims of prejudice. Few rose to the level of officer, black soldiers received three dollars less each month in pay than their white counterparts, and they were often given the most menial jobs. Yet blacks rushed to join the military, determined to fight against the South and slavery.

The Army of the Potomac

Following the victories of the Union Navy and Grant's army in the west, General McClellan finally took the offensive with his eastern army and headed for Richmond, Virginia, in June 1862. His forces were repulsed by Confederate General Robert E. Lee during a weeklong series of battles around Richmond. Then, on August 29, under the leadership of Henry Halleck and John Pope, the Union Army attacked the Confederates, who were led by Lee and Thomas "Stonewall" Jackson, a general whose fearlessness in the face of battle had earned him his nickname.

The fighting took place at Bull Run. It had been over a year since the First Battle of Bull Run, and the Union Army was in better condition. Still, it was no match for Lee's army, and it lost the Second Battle of Bull Run to the Confederates. Victorious, Lee and his army pushed farther north, hoping an invasion might convince the border states—those slave states that had

African-American soldiers served in many regiments for the Union Army. Seen here is the 26th United States Colored Volunteer Infantry.

remained in the Union—to join the Confederacy. In September, Lee's army invaded Maryland.

In nearby Washington, D.C., civilians feared that Lee's advancing army might invade the capital. Residents fled the city, leaving it deserted. There were rumors that the Confederate Army planned to occupy the White House and kidnap President Lincoln's wife and children. Military advisors asked the president's wife, Mary Todd Lincoln, to leave Washington with her children, but she refused to abandon the Union capital. As they continued their advance, Lee's troops met Union opposition and fell back to Sharpsburg, Maryland, where the Battle of Antietam began.

On September 16, 1862, Union troops under the command of Generals Joseph Hooker and Ambrose Burnside attacked Stonewall Jackson's men, who had hidden in the woods. The Battle of Antietam began in a cornfield near a small white church, then spread to a road later called Bloody Lane for all the men who were killed there. The battle finally ended at Antietam Creek. The Confederate forces controlled the lower bridge that spanned Antietam Creek, but General Burnside was determined that his men would get across. After many attempts, Burnside's men finally forced their way across the bridge, causing the Confederates to retreat. As soon as the Union men got across, though, Confederate reinforcements arrived. Burnside called for McClellan, whose troops were nearby, to reinforce him, but McClellan refused.

Burnside's men were forced to retreat over the bridge they had fought so hard to gain.

Although many looked at Antietam as a Union victory, it was not a decisive battle. Antietam was one of the costliest battles of the war. The Union suffered the greatest casualties, with a total of 12,401 dead or wounded, compared with the South's 10,318.[10] However, the Union Army had managed to stop Lee from proceeding farther north.

The Emancipation Proclamation

Considering Antietam a victory for the Union, President Lincoln chose this moment to take a step that he hoped would continue the momentum of victory, discourage foreign nations from entering the conflict between the states, and force the South into defeat. On September 22, 1862, shortly after Antietam, President Lincoln issued the preliminary Emancipation Proclamation. This proclamation, which would go into effect on January 1, 1863, freed the slaves in all the areas that continued to rebel against the United States. Slaves in states that had not seceded, or in states that had come under federal control, were not freed. Lincoln did not want to lose the support of the slave states that had sided with the Union, so he did not interfere with slavery there. He was eager to end the war, though, and he hoped that the seceding states might rejoin the Union in order to keep their slaves, at least temporarily.

This plan did not work. Even though the South valued its slaves very highly, it was willing to lose them in order to protect its right to self-rule. Though President Lincoln was personally opposed to slavery, his chief goal was to preserve the United States. Every action he took reflected this goal. "If I could save the Union without freeing *any* slave I would do it," Lincoln said in 1862. "and if I could save it by freeing all the slaves, I would do it; and if I could save it by freeing some and leaving others alone I would also do that."[11]

Drafting Men Into the Union Army

Other changes took place in the aftermath of the Battle of Antietam. The loss of so many Union soldiers at Antietam weakened morale in the North. Fewer men were volunteering for the army at a time when it desperately needed new recruits. In need of three hundred thousand more soldiers to replenish the Union Army, the United States government issued a conscription, or draft, law, in the summer of 1863. Previously, the country had relied strictly on volunteers to fill its military ranks.

After the passage of the law, federal enrolling officers compiled lists of eligible men, who were required to serve a three-year term. All those between the ages of twenty and forty-five were eligible. However, those who could afford to pay a $300 fee—a substantial sum at the time, greater than the average laborer's entire yearly salary—did not have to serve in the army.

SOURCE DOCUMENT

THAT ON THE 1ST DAY OF JANUARY, A.D. 1863, ALL PERSONS
HELD AS SLAVES WITHIN ANY STATE OR DESIGNATED PART OF
A STATE THE PEOPLE WHEREOF SHALL THEN BE IN
REBELLION AGAINST THE UNITED STATES SHALL BE THEN,
THENCEFORWARD, AND FOREVER FREE. . . .[12]

*President Abraham Lincoln issued the Emancipation
Proclamation in an attempt to encourage the states of
the Confederacy to come back to the Union with
slavery, at least temporarily.*

Neither did men who could afford to hire a substitute
to serve in their place, as 118,000 Union men did.[13]
Poor men, many of them recent immigrants, often
served as substitutes or were drafted.

Working-class people complained that the draft law
discriminated against the poor. Even Union soldiers
did not always approve of the conscription law.
Sergeant Samuel F. Hull was a mariner who had volunteered to serve with the 2nd Rhode Island. "I do not
believe in the proclamation of Lincoln in regard to the
300,000," he said of the conscription law, "Because it
does not give the poor man a chance. This is what
makes me down on our Government because our
Congressmen can pass laws and the poor man is not
much better than a dog."[14]

In New York, many working-class people opposed
the war and blamed Republicans for causing it. They
feared the Republican party was planning to flood

their cities with blacks after the war, taking jobs away from white workers. Northern Democrats opposed many of Lincoln's policies and questioned the constitutionality of actions like the draft law. In cities like Boston and New York, they staged protests against the conscription law. News of huge Union losses in battle also drummed up antiwar sentiment. In July 1863, New York City rioters stormed a provost marshal's office, hollering, "Down with the rich!" Any black people they encountered were attacked and beaten. For three days, the rioters continued to protest the war and the draft. They took out their frustrations on the black population, even burning down an orphanage for black children. Union troops were sent to New York to put down the riot.

Historians have long argued over the reasons for the Civil War. Some say it was fought over slavery. Others say it was fought over the conflicting issues of states' rights and the desire to preserve the Union. The people involved in the war brought their own reasons with them to the conflict, whether they were leaders, soldiers, or civilians on the home front.

THE HOME FRONT

Just two weeks after the Confederate attack on Fort Sumter, citizens in Windham County, Connecticut, drafted a resolution announcing that they "would expend their last dollar, and exhaust the last drop of their blood ere [before] they would submit to a disruption of the nation."[1] Windham County citizens pledged more than six thousand dollars for the Union cause at one mass meeting. Similar meetings were attended by citizens throughout the North who pledged their support, financially and emotionally, to the Union.

The Civil War mobilized the nation. Everywhere, people became involved in the war effort. Businesses teamed up with the government to produce weapons, ammunition, food, and supplies for the army. Women organized more than ten thousand soldiers' aid societies to help send clothing, food, medical supplies, and money to the troops. Organizations such as the Sanitary Commission and the Christian Commission worked to provide better conditions for soldiers. Children, old people, and women who were left at home worked to shoulder the burdens of running farms and businesses while the men were away fighting the war.

The Sanitary Commission

The United States Sanitary Commission (USSC), the primary civilian relief agency during the Civil War, was organized by Northerners after the attack on Fort Sumter. Originally called the Women's Central Association of Relief, the USSC was soon officially recognized by the government. It grew into a sprawling grassroots-supported organization with chapters in towns and cities across the North.

The United States Sanitary Commission, one of whose headquarters buildings is seen here, provided relief for the Union troops during the Civil War.

The USSC was dedicated to improving the welfare of the Union troops, who sometimes lived in unclean situations. Its main goal was to reduce the number of deaths due to disease among the Union ranks. The USSC employed inspectors who visited camps and hospitals, looking for ways to promote good health, good habits, and above all, cleanliness. USSC employees built latrines at soldiers' camps, washed clothes, provided food and bandages, and worked to keep the camps clean. Because of the USSC's efforts, a smaller percentage of soldiers died from disease during the Civil War than in previous wars. However, disease and accidents still claimed more lives than the battlefield did. A total of 224,000 Union soldiers died from disease or accidents during the Civil War, compared with the 140,000 Union troops who died in battle.[2]

Women such as Mary Ann Bickerdyke worked for the USSC on the front lines. Bickerdyke was a widow who traveled with the Union Army for four years, surviving nineteen battles. She fed, cleaned, clothed, and cared for the Union soldiers. Like other members of the USSC, Bickerdyke helped surgeons perform amputations on the wounded, and she washed soldiers' clothes in cauldrons of boiling water. When supplies were scarce, Bickerdyke went off by herself to forage in the countryside for food for the men, often bringing chickens and cattle back to camp with her. (Bickerdyke was not the only forager in the Union Army. Union soldiers themselves often raided the gardens and livestock left behind by fleeing Confederate civilians.) In addition to aiding and supplying the Union Army, the USSC transported and kept track of the wounded, created soldiers' homes where the wounded could recover after the war, and helped soldiers to receive their bounties and wages.

Among the items needed most by the USSC were condensed milk, beef stock, lemons, oranges, and cabbages; wines and liquors to soothe the injured; crutches for recovering amputees; and mattresses and beds for the wounded. Most of the USSC's volunteers were women affiliated with various soldiers' aid societies. They donated their time and labor to knit sweaters, socks, and caps; sew shirts; make jams and jellies; dry fruit; bake breads; and roll bandages—all of which were sent to USSC posts for distribution among the troops. USSC supplies were also distributed to Confederate prisoners of war.

Volunteer Effort

When they were not working or caring for their children, many Northern women volunteered their time to the war effort. Ladies' soldiers' aid societies in towns across the country produced clothing, food, and other useful items for soldiers. To understand how much time women spent making supplies to help the soldiers, consider the donations of one rural town. In the small town of Hubbardston, Massachusetts, women in the Ladies' Soldiers' Aid Society kept a list of all the packages they prepared and sent to soldiers on the field and in military hospitals during the Civil War. Between

1861 and 1865, the women of Hubbardston made or collected 109 bed quilts; 140 sheets; 18 blankets; 226 pillows; 30 pillowcases; 97 flannel shirts; 100 print shirts; 205 plain shirts; 93 pairs of underwear; 46 dressing gowns; 23 coats; 42 vests; 15 pairs of pants; 310 pairs of socks; 222 handkerchiefs; 31 pairs of slippers; 26 pairs of mittens; 166 towels; 42 napkins; 50 pin cushions; 50 comfort bags; 9 yards of netting; 7 pounds of cocoa; 51 pounds of cornstarch; 11 boxes of oatmeal; 5 large blocks of castille soap; and 64 bottles of blackberry cordial.[3]

Sanitary Fairs

To raise money and collect supplies, USSC volunteers held bazaars, musicals, lectures, and fairs in their towns. They also went door-to-door, asking for donations. Mary Livermore, the associate director of the Chicago branch of the USSC, came up with the idea of holding a sanitary fair on a grand scale. In 1863, she helped organize Chicago's "Great Northwest Fair," an elaborate exposition featuring livestock, produce, lectures, an art gallery, a curiosity shop, and a dining hall that could feed three thousand at one sitting. Merchants donated goods to be sold at the fair, farmers brought in wagonloads of produce, men donated a day's worth of wages, children donated their pennies, and women donated all kinds of handmade goods. The Great Northwest Fair went on for two weeks. It raised an astonishing $80,000 for the Union cause, an amount equivalent to about $1 million today.

Soon other cities held huge sanitary fairs, each one trying to outdo the other. Even children contributed to these fund-raisers. They picked peaches and blackberries that were later distributed to soldiers, and they made items to sell at the sanitary fairs. An entire wing of the 1864 New York sanitary fair was devoted to the sale of objects made by children such as the orphans of New York's "Home for the Friendless."[4] Children also formed their own groups, called Alert Clubs, which raised money for the USSC. The combined efforts of all the USSC workers and volunteers contributed more than $15 million worth of supplies to the Union cause during the Civil War.

Relief Agencies and Contrabands

Other relief agencies involved in the Civil War included the Christian Commission, organized by the Young Men's Christian Association (YMCA), and the New England Freedmen's Aid Society, which sent teachers and missionaries to the South to teach former slaves how to read and write. Tens of thousands of slaves were freed or left behind by their masters when plantation owners along the Carolina coast abandoned their properties to approaching Union troops.

Because Southerners had claimed these slaves as their property, slaves who crossed over to the Union lines became officially confiscated Confederate property. They were known as contrabands. (Contraband is property considered illegal during wartime that may be seized by government forces.) The contrabands were eager to become United States citizens. Many of them were unable to read or write, and hundreds of young Northern women jumped at the chance to teach them. Contrabands did not always have a means of making a living, so contraband relief agencies helped distribute supplies to them. The Union Army also hired many contrabands, some of whom were incorporated into African-American regiments. Many black soldiers were tutored by their officers or by civilian volunteers while they served in the army, and many learned to read and write.

In addition to those who volunteered to go to the front lines, there were many Northern civilians who

Contrabands were former slaves who fled to Union lines when the army approached. This family is fleeing behind Union lines in the hope of finding freedom.

unwittingly came into contact with Confederates in states such as Pennsylvania, which saw fighting between Union and Confederate forces. Patriotic Union citizens did their best to hinder the Confederates they met. Catharine Hunsecker, a German-American teenager, lived in Pennsylvania's Cumberland Valley during the Civil War. When Confederate soldiers began conducting raids in her community, searching for food, livestock, and other supplies, her family tried to hide their valuables. "When word first came that the 'Rebels' were coming . . . people generally started to hide their goods," Hunsecker remembered.

> . . . [T]he best of the horse gears were hidden in the bake oven. Some of the older and less valuable harness was allowed to remain in the usual place to avert suspicion that things were hidden away. Then the horses were taken away [hidden in the Cumberland Mountains] since the Confederates were known to be badly in need of horses and took all they could get.[5]

Women and Children at Work

Not all women involved in the war effort were nurses or USSC workers. A few determined women served as spies or soldiers during the Civil War. Frances Clalin served in the Union Army as a Missouri cavalry trooper, but she had to disguise herself as a man in order to join a regiment. Historians estimate that there may have been as many as four hundred women who fought in disguise as soldiers in the Union and Confederate armies during the Civil War.

Though neither side supported the idea of female soldiers, both the Union and the Confederacy used female spies to gather intelligence. Actress Pauline Cushman was in her twenties when she volunteered her services as a Union spy. Born in New Orleans, Cushman used her Southern heritage to convince Confederates to trust her. She was able to gather valuable information for the Union Army.

Women also worked on the front lines of the Civil War as postal employees. They operated out of tents that doubled as post offices. Both the Confederacy and the Union employed hundreds of women in the postal service. Female postal workers maintained communication lines and helped connect soldiers and their families while they were apart.

Receiving mail was so important to the soldiers that they sometimes cried when there was no letter for them at mail call. Soldiers often wrote home with news of other family members in the war, or news about other hometown men in their regiment. Mail traveled fairly rapidly through the Union lines and managed to reach soldiers in even the most remote locations. A Northern family might address a letter to their boy in uniform by including the names of his company, his regiment, and the division of the army in which he was serving, for example: "Private William Yank, 2nd Battalion, Company A, 124th New York Volunteers, serving in the 1st Brigade of the 2nd Division, III Corps of the Army of the Potomac."[6]

Pauline Cushman was one of the best known female spies for the Union.

When Union men went off to war, they left their farms and businesses behind. Women came forward to manage these operations in their absence. Farm women in the Midwest ran machinery and harvested crops themselves. In the cities, women worked in factories that churned out wartime supplies. The United States Treasury Department hired women to serve as clerks, because most male clerks had gone off to war. Women also did piecework at home for wages, usually sewing shirts and uniforms. Children also helped fill the jobs their fathers and older brothers had left behind. Boys in their early teens went to work in factories and mills, producing supplies for the war.

Grief and Loss

Aiding the war effort was one way for the millions of Americans on the home front to keep busy while waiting for news of loved ones fighting in the war. When casualty lists were released, people scanned them anxiously, hoping not to recognize any of the names. In the summer of 1863, Matilda Wentworth of Somersworth, New Hampshire, received a letter from her son Stephen. He wrote, "Mother, you must not worry about me. If I have got to die in battle or by sickness, no power on earth can help it. Remember that I stand as good a sight to return safe home as thousands of others."[7] One year later, on August 16, 1864, twenty-year-old Stephen was killed during fighting at Deep Bottom, Virginia. Mrs. Wentworth received

GEORGE'S TRUNK CAME UP EXPRESS EARLY IN FORENOON TODAY FROM CITY POINT, VIRGINIA. LIEUTENANT BABCOCK, OF THE 51ST, WAS KIND ENOUGH TO SEARCH IT OUT AND SEND IT HOME. IT STOOD SOME HOURS BEFORE WE FELT INCLINED TO OPEN IT. TOWARDS EVENING, MOTHER AND EDDY LOOKED OVER THE THINGS. ONE COULD NOT HELP FEELING DEPRESSED. THERE WERE HIS UNIFORM COAT, PANTS, SASH, ETC. THERE WERE MANY THINGS REMINDED US OF HIM. PAPERS, MEMORANDA, BOOKS, KNICK-KNACKS, A REVOLVER, A SMALL DIARY, ROLL OF HIS COMPANY, A CASE OF PHOTOGRAPHS OF HIS COMRADES (SEVERAL OF THEM I KNEW AS KILLED IN BATTLE), WITH OTHER STUFF SUCH AS A SOLDIER ACCUMULATES.... WE HAVE NOT HEARD FROM HIM SINCE OCTOBER 3RD, EITHER LIVING OR DEAD, WE KNOW NOT.[8]

Missing relatives who were off fighting the war took a hard toll on civilians. This piece by poet Walt Whitman illustrates the hardships American families went through during the war.

a letter from the United States Army, telling her of his death.

Many families experienced the loss of a loved one during the Civil War. Asa and Submit Moulton of North Brookfield, Massachusetts, lost both of their sons in the war. Their twenty-two-year-old son, David, was killed in the Battle of Fredericksburg in 1862. Their eighteen-year-old son, Henry, starved to death in Andersonville Prison, a Confederate jail for Union prisoners that became notorious for its terrible conditions, in 1865. Because the different companies of a regiment were often organized locally, it was not unusual for one town to lose many of its young men during the war. The town of Woodstock, Connecticut, lost one third of all the soldiers it sent to the war. Another 20 percent of the soldiers from Woodstock were wounded, and 18 percent were captured.[9] Local soldiers' aid societies often continued to hold fundraisers after the war until they had raised enough money to erect a monument to the town's veterans, both living and dead.

The war was especially hard on those who had loved ones on both sides of the conflict. Katherine Hubbell was a Connecticut woman who married a man from Georgia in 1860. When the Civil War broke out one year later, her husband and brothers-in-law fought for the Confederacy, while her own brother fought for the Union. Countless individuals endured this same hardship. Even President Lincoln's wife, Mary Todd Lincoln of Kentucky, had relatives on both sides of the war. Some of her brothers fought and died for the Confederacy, whereas others fought for the Union.

Government and Business

The Civil War created an unprecedented partnership between the federal government and Northern industry. To streamline business and government transactions, Congress created a national banking system that enforced the use of one national currency instead of the many different currencies that had been used before the war. The War Department spent hundreds of millions of tax dollars to supply Union armed forces with ships, weapons, ammunition, horses, uniforms, boots, tents, blankets, food, medicine, and other supplies. The partnership between private industry and the War Department ensured that these necessary items would be produced. Shoe factories set to work producing thousands of pairs of boots for the army, woolen mills churned out blankets, and meat manufacturers such as Philip Armour produced dried and pickled meat for army rations. Samuel Colt ran his arms factory day and night to make revolvers for the Union Army. Button manufacturers churned out buttons for military uniforms.

Many businesses were revived by the frenzy of wartime spending. The railroad industry thrived, thanks to increased freight. Woolen mills made huge profits from increased production and sales. The town of Springfield, Massachusetts, site of a United States

Armory, boomed during the war. Armory employees increased more than tenfold, and the number of rifles manufactured there jumped from a low of 800 per month in 1861 to a high of 26,000 per month in 1864.[10]

Not all the products created by Northern industry were well made, however. At the beginning of the war, a number of money-hungry businessmen took the War Department's money and delivered shoddy products— shoes that fell apart on the first wearing, blankets that were too thin to keep anyone warm, and food that was spoiled. Some businessmen raised their prices, forcing the country to buy their goods at an inflated rate in order to increase their personal gain.

Paying for the War

To pay for the enormous cost of the war, the government issued war bonds and levied new taxes, including the first income tax on the wealthy in United States history. In addition to paying federal taxes, many Americans also paid higher town taxes in order to cover the cost of the war. Across the country, towns voted to help support the families of soldiers while they were away, as well as to reward each man who volunteered for the war. In 1861, townspeople in Woodstock, Connecticut, agreed to pay $1.50 a week to the wives of volunteers and fifty cents a week for each child of theirs who was under the age of fourteen. By 1862, Woodstock was offering volunteers fifty dollars to join the army. By 1863, that amount had increased to one hundred fifty dollars.

As the war dragged on, it became more difficult to recruit new men into the army. In some areas, new recruits were paid bounties as high as one thousand dollars in order to encourage them to join the army. Some men, known as bounty jumpers, profited from the bounty system. They signed up for military service in a town that offered a high bounty, collected the money, and then disappeared, without ever reporting for service. By 1863, it had become very difficult for towns to enroll new recruits. The optimism and excitement that had led so many young men to enlist in the early days of the war had evaporated as Union losses mounted and casualty lists grew. Americans began to wonder whether the war would ever end.

I have been in the service now for two years and the war is no nearer to a close than it was when it first commenced," wrote Sergeant Samuel F. Hull in the spring of 1863: "Been through all sorts of hardships all for nothing. . . . I look at this war as a prolonged war."[1]

STRUGGLING TO WIN

The Struggle to Find a Leader

As the war dragged on, it continued to take a heavy toll on the Union as well as the Confederacy. The Union was particularly troubled by a lack of effective military leadership. Disappointed by many of the Union Army's generals, President Lincoln repeatedly replaced hesitant leaders, such as George McClellan, with ones he hoped would be better. To enhance his understanding of military strategy, the president stayed up late at night, reading books on military science.

Meanwhile, fighting between Lee's and Burnside's armies continued in December 1862 at Fredericksburg, Virginia, where the North suffered extreme losses. In March 1863, Lee's army attacked Union forces commanded by Joseph Hooker in Chancellorsville,

Virginia, forcing a Union retreat after Hooker lost an astonishing seventeen thousand men.

So many Union soldiers died during the war that there were not enough cemeteries to hold them all. New ones had to be built. Union and Confederate regiments usually collected their dead after a battle and gave them a proper military burial. "When a man dies he is at once reported to his Captain who details a squad of his company to dig the grave," explained Solomon Stocker of the 30th Ohio Volunteer Infantry:

> The interment is usually made the same day of the death or early the following day. The corpse is carried on stretcher and in absence of coffin (usually no coffin) is wrapt in blanket, body dressed in common soldier suit. While moving to the grave solemn martial music is played. Sometimes the presence of a Chaplain solemnizes the occasion. . . . The firing of three vollies over the corpse or grave is an act intended [to give] the last earthly honors to [the] departed one. Often there is not an eye present to shed a tear. The tear must be shed far away.[2]

Individual burials were not always possible. When there were massive numbers of dead whose identities were unknown, the fallen soldiers were often buried in a shallow mass grave. Sometimes these graves bore no markers at all. Other times, a wooden sign was erected, telling the number of men buried and whether they were Union or Confederate soldiers. Music was often a part of military burials, and it also played an important role in other aspects of the military.

Marching Songs and Battle Hymns

Military leaders know that morale is essential to the success of any army. In order to improve morale among soldiers in the Civil War, both the Union and Confederate armies had their own repertoire of music. Regimental bands often played marching songs and battle tunes to help pass the time and make the men step a little quicker as the units moved from place to place. Music helped make marches, which could be as long as twenty-five miles at one time, bearable.

One of the most popular Union songs, called "John Brown's Body," was about the abolitionist John Brown, who had dedicated his life to ending slavery. The song went, "John Brown's body lies a-moldering in the grave, but his soul goes marching on. . . ."[3]

Julia Ward Howe, a poet and abolitionist from Boston, heard the Union troops singing this song while she was visiting Washington, D.C., in 1861. It inspired her to write a song to the same tune. She called it "The Battle Hymn of the Republic." Howe's song insisted that God was on the side of the North, and it quickly became a hit with the Union troops. "He has sounded forth the trumpet that shall never sound retreat," went the song, "his truth is marching on."[4] This song inspired many Union soldiers not to give up.

The Siege of Vicksburg

The Northern strategy in the Civil War had always been to cut the South in half. President Lincoln had long believed that, regardless of what happened in the East, the war could not be won until Vicksburg, Mississippi, which lay on the Mississippi River, was captured. Vicksburg was a stronghold for the Confederacy. Because it was a port city, much of the food, blankets, ammunition, and other supplies needed by the Confederate Army were shipped from there.

Union General Ulysses S. Grant developed a daring plan for Vicksburg's capture. Instead of attacking the city directly and predictably, Grant had General William Tecumseh Sherman fake an attack to distract the Confederates. Meanwhile, Grant and his men moved in a counterclockwise circle, finally approaching Vicksburg from the east and laying siege to the city. Grant's army surrounded the city, cutting off all supplies and shelling it repeatedly. Still, the citizens of Vicksburg refused to surrender. They dug caves under the ground and burrowed into them. Vicksburg slowly ran out of food, and its citizens began to slaughter their horses and mules for food. To stave off hunger, some resorted to eating rats. Even so, they did not surrender.

A Soldier's Diet

Wherever it went, the Union Army was supplied by railroad or wagon train. The Confederate Army did not have as many resources, and it was often sorely lacking in basic supplies and foodstuffs.

Today, the United States military has special meals for its troops to eat in the field. At the time of the Civil War, however, the only means of preserving food was

Union General Ulysses S. Grant hoped that, by capturing the port city of Vicksburg, Mississippi, he would divide and conquer the Confederacy.

by salting, pickling, canning, or drying. Soldiers often had to eat rations that were spoiled or crawling with bugs. Union Army rations consisted of beans, bacon, pickled beef, dried vegetables, hardtack (a cracker that was good for traveling because it did not crumble or spoil easily), and coffee. Occasionally, the soldiers might have a treat such as fresh oysters or fruit, but at other times, they might run out of food or have to eat the same thing for weeks.

Not everyone stayed healthy on Union rations. "Charley, do not enlist," Stephen J. Wentworth of the 4th New Hampshire Volunteers warned his brother.

> Stay at home and remain so. If you come out here you would not stand one chance in ten in remaining well. There are a great many sick in the regiment. Our principal living is hard tack and fried salt pork. The hard tack is so hard that we have to soak it to make it soft so we can eat it. About once a week, and sometimes oftener we get fresh beef, and an occasional soup. The coffee is not fit to drink, at least I can't drink it. I have not drank three dippers of coffee since I enlisted. I have often made a meal on hard tack and water, but it agrees with me.[5]

Poor diet probably contributed to the high number of soldiers who died from sickness and disease during the war.

Because the Civil War also brought men from many different backgrounds together into close quarters, the soldiers were exposed to new diseases to which they had no immunity. Farmers made up half of the army. Many of them had lived in isolated rural areas where they were not exposed to diseases often found in urban areas. Thus, soldiers from the Midwest, which was relatively rural, were 43 percent more likely to die of disease than soldiers from the more densely populated and urban Northeast.[6]

Gettysburg

In the summer of 1863, while Ulysses S. Grant and his men surrounded the city of Vicksburg, Mississippi, and attempted to starve it into submission, General Robert E. Lee launched a second invasion of the North. Lee's army marched north unopposed until it surprised Union forces at Gettysburg, Pennsylvania, on July 1, 1863. Both sides immediately sent for reinforcements and awaited their arrival.

By the morning of July 2, eighty-five thousand Union forces had gathered in a line along Cemetery Ridge, which had two hills on either end of it. The hills on the northern end of Cemetery Ridge were called Cemetery Hill and Culp's Hill. The hills on the southern end were called Big Round Top and Little Round Top.

Some sixty-five thousand Confederates had arranged themselves parallel to the Union line, along a lower elevation known as Seminary Ridge. General Lee decided that the best tactic would be to divide his army in two, take the offensive, and storm the Union line at the hills on its ends. The Union men, led by General George Meade, were ordered to defend their positions at all costs. But one Union general, Daniel

Sickles, whom Meade had assigned to defend Little Round Top, had his own idea. He moved his men away from Little Round Top, toward the Confederate line. This move left Little Round Top exposed and undefended. Discovering that Sickles was out of position, General Meade ordered him back into place, but before he could return to Little Round Top, the attack had already begun. The Confederates saw where the Union line was weakest, and they began climbing Little Round Top. Meade realized that the Battle of Gettysburg now hinged on control of Little Round Top. If the Confederates took control of the hill, they would be able to take aim at the entire Union line along Cemetery Ridge.

In desperate straits, Meade immediately ordered in reinforcements for Little Round Top. Chief among these reinforcements was the 20th Maine, a 350-man regiment composed of loggers, river drivers, fishermen, and farmers. Their captain was a young college professor named Joshua Lawrence Chamberlain. The fate of the Union Army at Gettysburg now in its hands, the 20th Maine took its position on Little Round Top just as the 15th Alabama reached the top of the hill. For over an hour, the two regiments battled, and Chamberlain lost a third of his men. Then, just as the 20th Maine was outnumbered and running short of ammunition, Chamberlain ordered an unorthodox but effective maneuver. With Confederates rapidly advancing on Little Round Top, Chamberlain had the right flank of his Maine men remain in position while he ordered

Some of the most desperate fighting in the Battle of Gettysburg took place as the opposing forces tried to take hold of Little Round Top, seen here just after the battle.

the left flank to swing down the hill like a giant door on its hinge. The left flank then swung back up the hill toward the right flank. This move confused and frightened the Alabama regiment, which began to retreat. The men of the 20th Maine managed to hold Little Round Top.

Though it managed to hold its positions, the Union Army had suffered severe losses. Eighty-two percent of the 1st Minnesota fell when the regiment charged a group of Confederates six times its size in order to seal a gap in the Union defenses on Cemetery

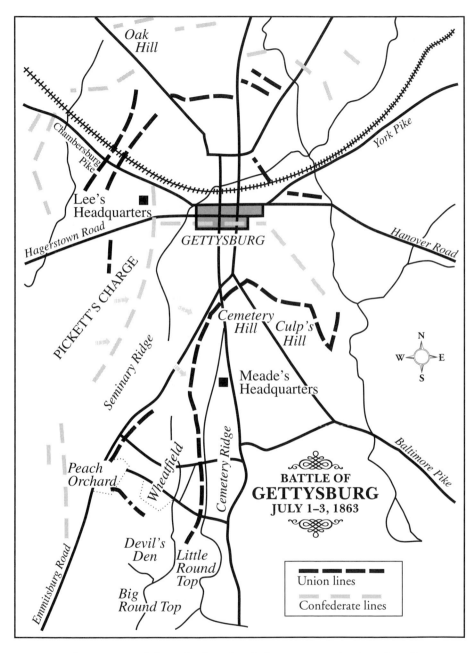

The Union defeated the Confederates at the Battle of
Gettysburg, but both sides had lost so many soldiers that it
was not an overwhelming victory.

Ridge. On the final day of fighting at Gettysburg, Lee ordered Confederate General James Longstreet to attack the Union center with three divisions, including General George Pickett's. As they charged, Pickett's men were decimated by Union forces, who fired at them from behind the safety of a stone wall. Thus, Gettysburg ended with a devastating loss for the Confederates. The Union Army was victorious, but it had suffered twenty-three thousand casualties. The Confederates sustained twenty-eight thousand casualties.[7]

One third of the men who fought at Gettysburg were killed. The town of Gettysburg became one giant hospital for the wounded. Later, a Union cemetery was created at Gettysburg to commemorate those who had given their lives there. President Lincoln dedicated this new cemetery on November 19, 1863, with the delivery of his now-famous Gettysburg Address.

Military Hospitals and Women Nurses

Almost every regiment had a field surgeon or a hospital steward who operated out of tents, caring for the regiment's wounded in field hospitals. In addition, there were more than three thousand women who worked as army nurses for the Union, earning forty cents a day.[8] Nurses often put their lives in danger by working on or near the front lines of battle.

Dorothea Dix, a pioneer in the effort to reform hospitals for the mentally ill, was appointed by the United States Army to oversee its nurses. The military did not think it was a good idea for attractive young women to act as nurses and mix with the soldiers, so Dix was firm about the kind of women she wanted for army nurses. She preferred to hire serious women over the age of thirty who were plain-looking rather than beautiful. Dix also insisted that army nurses wear dark-colored dresses with no jewelry or bows.

One of the most famous Civil War nurses was Clara Barton, a young woman from Oxford, Massachusetts, who became known as the Angel of the Battlefield. Barton left her job as a clerk in the United States Patent Office to help the Union Army. She organized supply wagons and saw that necessary items such as medicine, soap, food, cups, and blankets made it to the places they were needed most. She fearlessly tended the wounded, putting their well-being above her own. Barton recalled that after one battle, her skirt was so soaked with the blood of the wounded, she had to wring it out in order to be able to walk. After the war, Barton continued to assist the army in identifying the dead and setting up cemeteries. She later helped found the American Red Cross.

Whenever possible, wounded soldiers were trans-ported from makeshift field hospitals to stationary hospitals such as the Armory Square Hospital in Washington, D.C. There, they would either die or recover. If they recovered, there was a good chance that they would be returned to their regiment. Even soldiers who had not fully recovered were kept in an Invalid Corps, and they might be asked to help out. As

Clara Barton, often called the "Angel of the Battlefield," was perhaps the most famous Union nurse during the Civil War.

the war dragged on, the Union ran out of hospital space and had to erect makeshift outdoor hospitals to accommodate the growing number of wounded.

For the injured, life was painful and often brief. Antibiotics had not been discovered yet. In fact, people at the time did not thoroughly understand the ways in which germs spread illness. Surgical tools were not sterile. Neither were bandages. Doctors did the best they could, but they had little to offer their patients. Chloroform gas was used as a painkiller, but it was not always available. Amputations were common. If an arm or leg became severely infected, the remedy was usually to cut off the limb before the infection could spread to the rest of the body.

The Union victory at Gettysburg in 1863 was followed by the surrender of Vicksburg to Grant's army on the Fourth of July, 1863. The hungry Confederate Army in Vicksburg had finally given up. After being taken prisoner, the Confederate soldiers were treated humanely and fed United States government hardtack. Not all prisoners of war were so lucky. For many Union soldiers held in Confederate prison camps, there was little or nothing to eat.

Prisoners of War

Civilian prisoners of war were treated very differently from soldiers who were taken prisoner. Southern civilians taken prisoner by the Union Army were often released after they agreed to swear an oath of loyalty to the Union. "You would be surprised to see the

Secession prisoners here," wrote one Union soldier who was stationed in Virginia:

> Some tolerably fine looking young women swear most woefully. . . . We are obliged to take some women prisoners as well as the men for they are even more dangerous. Many of these men and women, after staying a few days in prison, are willing to take the Union Oath and are then allowed to return home.[9]

For soldiers, imprisonment was much harsher. At the Rock Island, Illinois, federal prison camp, eighteen hundred Confederate prisoners died from a smallpox epidemic. At Libby Prison in Richmond, Virginia, thirteen hundred Union soldiers were housed in just six rooms. One of the worst prison camps of the war was the one for Union captives in Andersonville, Georgia.

Andersonville Prison in Georgia was the largest Confederate prison for Union prisoners of war. As many as thirty-two thousand Union soldiers were kept there at one time. More than half of them starved to death or died from disease. The South, short of food and supplies for its own men, spared nothing on Union prisoners. Andersonville Prison covered twenty-six swampy acres of ground that had been specially selected by the prison commander, Captain Henry Wirz, because the area seemed likely to promote ill health. Thousands of men were packed into this enclosure with no shelter from the sun or rain, and with no place to go to the bathroom except the swamp itself. They were not allowed any water, and thus were forced to drink the polluted ooze of the swamp. If any men tried to escape, they were immediately shot by prison guards. As many as one hundred Union men died in Andersonville each day.

Twenty-year-old Charles Ferren Hopkins was captured by Confederates in the spring of 1864. "Inside the camp," wrote Hopkins, "death stalked on every hand. Death at the hand of the guards, th[r]ough murder in cold blood, was merciful beside the systematic, absolute murder inside, by slow death, inch by inch!"[10]

Hopkins lived to tell his story of Andersonville. Others were not so lucky. Thirty-year-old Timothy McCarthy, an immigrant from Cork County, Ireland, who joined the 25th Massachusetts, was taken prisoner at Cold Harbor, Virginia, and died in Andersonville Prison four months later. Sergeant Ichabod Corbin

This 1864 photograph shows Union troops heading into battle.

Davis of the 18th Connecticut managed to survive nine months of starvation and neglect in Andersonville Prison, but collapsed and died while walking to the rescue boat after the camp was liberated by the Union Army.[11]

Union Defeats

In September 1863, Union troops led by General William Rosecrans were defeated at the bloody Battle of Chickamauga in Georgia. More fighting followed in Chattanooga, Tennessee, where Generals Grant and William Tecumesh Sherman won a victory for the Union in November. The war dragged on into 1864. In May of that year, Generals Grant and Meade marched their armies toward the Confederate capital of Richmond, Virginia. The bloodiest weeks of the war were about to begin.

As many as two thousand Union men were wounded each day during the Virginia campaign. In May and June, the Union Army was defeated by Lee's army three times: at the Battle of the Wilderness, the Battle of Spotsylvania, and the Battle of Cold Harbor. At Cold Harbor, the Union suffered between five thousand and seven thousand casualties during the first eight minutes of fighting. Northern critics called Grant a butcher because he was willing to sacrifice so many of his own men to win a battle. Despite tremendous losses, the Grand Army of the Republic, as the Union troops were called, continued to push farther south into Virginia.

Bolstered by ample supplies, which were brought in by railroad car and steamship, the Union Army was able to continue to fight. The Confederacy, in contrast, was fast running out of both soldiers and supplies. Because it had far fewer factories and mills than the North, the Confederacy was hard-pressed to produce the volume of goods needed to supply its army. It did not have enough food or uniforms to feed and clothe its soldiers. Many Confederate soldiers went barefoot.

With a much smaller white male population than the North, the Confederacy also began to run out of able-bodied men who could serve as soldiers. Though it had many male slaves, the Confederacy did not dare arm them for fear they might turn against their white owners. In some cases, the Confederate Army resorted to using older men and young boys to bolster its army. This created resentment among the Southern people, some of whom began to believe that the well-being of their families was more important than the cause of the Confederacy.

Waiting It Out

In June 1864, the Union Army laid siege to the town of Petersburg, Virginia, where Lee's army had taken refuge. Union troops dug a network of trenches around Petersburg and lived in them while they shelled the town. For ten months, Petersburg held out.

Boredom was a constant problem for soldiers during sieges or any other time when they waited for action. Some soldiers played cards or drank liquor, if it was allowed, to pass the time. All soldiers were thrilled to receive a letter or package from friends and family. "Send papers and books as often as you can, for they serve to while away the long evenings," Private Stephen J. Wentworth wrote home to his parents.

> We are not allowed to go to bed until after roll call (nine o'clock). I don't think it is a good plan to send tracts and religious papers out here to the boys, for they never read them. They want something exciting. It is impossible to sit down out here in the midst of a group of noisy boys and settle your mind enough to enjoy religious reading. Not that I find fault with it, but to let you know that the boys do not think anything of a parcel of religious tracts and papers. It is useless to send them. They are only thrown away. A great many of our boys are very homesick. I am contented, do not want to go home until the war is over, only I should like to see you all first rate.[12]

Union and Confederate soldiers were often camped so close that they could talk to each other, exchange goods, or even play games. Communication between the opposite sides was against orders, but officers sometimes looked the other way. "Yesterday morning . . . one of the 'Johnnies' (a name which the rebs always go by) crowed like a rooster," wrote one officer:

> One of our boys answered back, which soon led to talking between them. It was agreed to exchange papers. I saw the boy was anxious to exchange so I went off out of the way, for it is against orders to talk or exchange articles with the enemy. . . . [T]he men are not particular whether they break orders or not, as long as they are not caught.[13]

The Union and Confederate soldiers were sometimes willing to socialize with one another. Yet it was understood that they would also fire on one another when ordered to do so.

The Road to Victory

While the two armies were squared off at Petersburg, Union General William Tecumseh Sherman's western army, composed primarily of men from Ohio, Indiana, Pennsylvania, and Tennessee, was on the move. Starting from Chattanooga, Tennessee, in May 1864, it marched toward Atlanta, fighting off the Confederate Army as it approached. Cutting off all supplies into Atlanta, Sherman's men starved the city out. By the end of September, the once proud Southern city had fallen into Union hands.

Sherman's campaign in the South was intended to subdue the Confederacy not just through military strength, but also through humiliation. As Union soldiers marched through Southern territory, they burned buildings, raided homes, and tore up railroad tracks, inflicting a terrible blow to Southern morale. Sherman hoped that the devastation wrought by Union soldiers would help cripple the Confederacy emotionally as well as physically, and thus bring the war closer to an end. Sherman's army captured Savannah, Georgia; Columbia, South Carolina; and, by the spring of 1865, Raleigh, North Carolina.

The army grew as it moved through the South; thousands of slaves left their masters and marched with the Union Army. Sherman's march through Confederate territory was tremendously demoralizing to Southern civilians. Sherman's army lived off the land as it marched through the South, pillaging homes and destroying factories, public buildings, railroads, and bridges. Meanwhile, the North carried on. In January 1865, Congress had approved the Thirteenth Amendment to the Constitution, which, after its ratification in December 1865, would abolish slavery in the United States.

In March 1865, nearly a year after the Union Army had begun the siege at Petersburg, the standoff ended. To prevent the Confederate Army from being encircled by encroaching federal troops, General Lee ordered it to abandon its position at Petersburg. As the Confederates headed west, the city of Richmond fell to the Union. Throughout the North, citizens celebrated the fall of the Confederate capital. Bells rang out in cities, newspapers printed extra editions to announce the news, and people rushed into the streets to celebrate. With great relief, they sensed that the end of the war was near.

Surrender at Appomattox

On April 9, 1865, Grant's army cornered Lee and his men at the town of Appomattox Court House, Virginia. Lee surrendered his army to Grant, marking the approaching end of the Civil War. Once again, celebration broke out in the North.

Union General William Tecumseh Sherman became famous for his march through Georgia and his burning of several major Southern cities.

President Lincoln requested that a band play the Southern song "Dixie," in an effort to reach out to the surrendered Confederacy. With the immense relief that came as peace approached, Lincoln told his wife that he was now happier than he had ever been.[14]

Five days later, on the evening of April 14, 1865, as Abraham and Mary Todd Lincoln held hands inside their box at Ford's Theatre in Washington, D.C., a man named John Wilkes Booth shot President Lincoln in the back of the head. The following morning, Abraham Lincoln died. He was the first United States president to die at the hand of an assassin.

Across the North, the Union mourned. Buildings were draped with black cloth, and mourners came out to watch the president's funeral train as it passed through their city on its way to Illinois. Excitement over the end of the Civil War was now muted by a deep sadness.

"Can it be that our much loved and honored President Lincoln is—dead," wrote twenty-two-year-old Julia Peter to her fiancé, who was marching with Sherman's army:

> Oh! It seems impossible. . . . Only a few days ago we were all so happy and rejoicing over our brilliant success. Now all is sorrow and gloom and on the very day—which, to us here, was to be a day of joy and thanksgiving for our blessings, our victories—we are mourning. . . . Oh! Must we not think that God has sent this as a judgement upon us, for our sins against Him? . . . We are all so sad today.[15]

Going Home

On May 23, 1865, the Grand Army of the Potomac began its march down Pennsylvania Avenue in Washington, D.C. Celebrating crowds of onlookers cheered them and sang patriotic songs. Reviewing the troops from the White House were newly sworn-in President Andrew Johnson and General Ulysses S. Grant. The procession went on for two days as some one hundred fifty thousand soldiers marched through Washington. They were homeward bound, waiting to board the trains and steamships that would carry them back to their home states and to their families.

At long last, the war was over. Victory had been costly. Northern soldiers, as well as the president of the United States, had paid for it with their lives. But the Union had been preserved.

The Civil War claimed the lives of 624,000 Americans, both north and south. This is more people than were killed in every other American war, before Vietnam, combined. Another half a million Americans were wounded in the war but survived. The effects of the Civil War

RECONSTRUCTING THE UNION

on the United States were devastating. More than 2 million men had served in the Union Army, and each family left behind by a soldier was affected by his absence. The Civil War cost the nation an estimated $20 billion—and in addition to this financial cost, there was the huge emotional cost paid by those who lost loved ones in a war fought not with a foreign enemy, but with fellow countrymen.

The Civil War transformed the United States. For many white Southerners, it brought an end to a way of life. For former slaves, the Civil War was a turning point that granted them greater freedom than they had ever known, though they were still a long way from achieving racial equality. The Civil War had also given women a chance to prove themselves equal to men on the front lines and the home front. In fact, the Civil

SOURCE DOCUMENT

(3—040.)

RECORD DIVISION

ACKNOWLEDGING RECEIPT OF CLAIM.

℗ DEPARTMENT OF THE INTERIOR,
BUREAU OF PENSIONS,
Washington, D. C., _May_ 7, 188 8.

Sir: Your claim for pension has been received, recorded, and given a number as below, and will be taken up for action in its regular turn. The intervening time can be employed in preparing necessary evidence.

Your claim is entitled _____ No. 642414 _____

Private Co. 2" R. D. Inf. +

____ x ____ Co. ____ 2" Battln V.R.C.,

and in all communications relative thereto be sure and state the same in full, as above. Very respectfully,

John C. Black Com.

(10802—50 M.) 6—186

The war cost an enormous amount in both money and lives. Even after the war ended, there were costs to be paid, in the form of pensions for soldiers who had fought for the Union.

War activities of women helped lay the groundwork for the women's suffrage movement. Many women who had been involved in the war effort turned their energies toward achieving equality for women after the war. Men's lives changed, too. Returning soldiers who had traveled far and seen many different regions of the country were less likely to want to stay home on the farm after the war. Many of them packed up and moved west with their families, seeking a new life and new opportunities.

The role of the government in people's lives also expanded as a result of the Civil War. The federal government of the United States, which so many men had given their lives to preserve, now assumed a greater role. The power of the state governments, on the other hand, was diminished. During the war, the federal government had levied the first national income tax as well as a national draft. After the war, as the government administered veteran's benefits and freedmen's aid and restored order to the war-torn South, it continued to maintain an active presence in people's everyday lives.

Reconstruction

After the Civil War, the federal government set about the task of rebuilding the South, which included punishing those who had sided with the Confederacy against the Union. Leading this government was President Andrew Johnson. Drastic changes took place in the Southern states as the United States tried to enforce national rule and increase racial equality there.

Congress decided not to readmit the seceding states until they had ratified the Fourteenth Amendment to the Constitution, which established the supremacy of the federal government over the individual states. The Fourteenth Amendment did not expressly grant black men the right to vote, but it did reward states that chose to extend voting rights to black men by increasing those states' representation in Congress. States that refused to allow black men to vote had their representation decreased proportionally. The Fourteenth Amendment also denied prominent Confederate leaders the right to hold high office in the United States.

Not surprisingly, most of the existing legislatures in the Southern states refused to ratify the Fourteenth Amendment. Disagreements over how to deal with former Confederates and how best to bring the South back into the Union caused so much disagreement among political leaders that President Johnson, who opposed the Fourteenth Amendment, was impeached in the House of Representatives in 1868. Johnson was not convicted by the Senate, however, so he was never removed from office. But much of the Congress was unhappy with his leadership.

The Radical Republicans

Northern representatives in Congress were known as Radical Republicans because they hoped to change the South drastically to help secure the rights of the former slaves. They were upset by Johnson's Reconstruction policies, which were inconsistent and seemed to favor wealthy white planters at the expense of free blacks.

At first, Johnson had decided that some Southerners, including high-level Confederate officials, would be barred from holding public office. Later, Johnson pardoned many of these individuals and allowed them to run for office. Once elected, these Southerners passed laws that discriminated against the former slaves, making it difficult for them to live as free citizens. And although the Union had set aside many abandoned Southern plantations during the Civil War as land for former slaves to resettle on temporarily, President Johnson decided that the land

Andrew Johnson, who became president after Lincoln's assassination, faced a battle with Congress over how Reconstruction should proceed.

should go back to its previous owners, who were white planters. Decisions like these angered Radical Republicans, who feared Johnson was trying to recreate the South the way it was before the war.

To speed up Reconstruction in the South, Congress passed the Military Reconstruction Act in 1867. Under this act, the old governments in the South were dissolved and the federal military was authorized to run the South until new governments could be elected. The Military Reconstruction Act also forced the South to ratify the Fourteenth Amendment and to allow blacks the right to vote. In addition, it barred all prominent Confederates from participating in government. To enforce this act and maintain order, federal troops were stationed in the South.

Other Reconstruction efforts focused on helping Southerners recover from the war. To assist former slaves, the federal government established the Freedmen's Bureau, which distributed food to needy blacks and whites. The Freedmen's Bureau also helped former slaves disentangle themselves from their former masters and worked to educate blacks. However, because many impoverished former slaves did not have land of their own to work, it was very hard for them to improve their lives. Many ended up working on the same plantations they had lived on as slaves. The only difference was that the white land owners paid them— generally very poorly—for their work.

Military courts were set up to deal with criminals in the South. Captain Henry Wirz, the infamous

THE THIRTEENTH AMENDMENT

SECTION 1. NEITHER SLAVERY NOR INVOLUNTARY SERVITUDE, EXCEPT AS PUNISHMENT FOR CRIME WHEREOF THE PARTY SHALL HAVE BEEN DULY CONVICTED, SHALL EXIST WITHIN THE UNITED STATES, OR ANY PLACE SUBJECT TO THEIR JURISDICTION.

THE FOURTEENTH AMENDMENT

SECTION 1. ALL PERSONS BORN OR NATURALIZED IN THE UNITED STATES, AND SUBJECT TO THE JURISDICTION THEREOF, ARE CITIZENS OF THE UNITED STATES AND OF THE STATE WHEREIN THEY RESIDE. NO STATE SHALL MAKE OR ENFORCE ANY LAW WHICH SHALL ABRIDGE THE PRIVILEGES OR IMMUNITIES OF CITIZENS OF THE UNITED STATES; NOR SHALL ANY STATE DEPRIVE ANY PERSON OF LIFE, LIBERTY, OR PROPERTY, WITHOUT DUE PROCESS OF THE LAW; NOR DENY TO ANY PERSON WITHIN ITS JURISDICTION THE EQUAL PROTECTION OF THE LAWS.

FIFTEENTH AMENDMENT

SECTION 1. THE RIGHT OF CITIZENS OF THE UNITED STATES TO VOTE SHALL NOT BE DENIED OR ABRIDGED BY THE UNITED STATES OR BY ANY STATE ON ACCOUNT OF RACE, COLOR, OR PREVIOUS CONDITION OF SERVITUDE.[1]

The Thirteenth, Fourteenth, and Fifteenth amendments to the United States Constitution are known collectively as the Civil War amendments. They were designed to give the former slaves civil rights.

commander of the Andersonville Prison camp, was convicted of murder and hanged. Yet many other Southerners went unpunished.

Reconstruction policies tried to stimulate industry in the war-torn Southern states and promote business enterprises. As the South was rebuilt, railroad, construction, and banking businesses flourished. Many Northerners moved to the South to take advantage of these new business opportunities. Known as carpetbaggers because of the popular cloth-covered suitcases they carried, these people were generally disliked by Southerners, who did not want to see Northern businessmen profit from the defeat of the South.

Though Reconstruction policies were created with the best of intentions, corruption and greed often got in the way of carrying them out. Many Southerners were unwilling to give up the ways of the old South. Thus black Americans did not achieve equality easily.

The Civil War split the country apart, and in the end, it brought a divided nation back together. Though the war wrought tremendous change in the United States, it could not change the attitudes of Americans overnight. The new Union continued to experience problems of unrest and civil division, but—armed with the memory of the terrible conflict that had pitted countryman against countryman—its leaders and citizens were determined to face the future as a united front.

★ TIMELINE ★

1787—Delegates to the Constitutional Convention create the Three-Fifths Compromise to deal with slavery in the United States.

1816—The American Colonization Society is formed to send freed slaves back to Africa.

1820—The Missouri Compromise bans slavery in the Louisiana Purchase territory north of the 36th parallel.

1830—Senators Daniel Webster and Robert Hayne argue over states' rights and the authority of the federal government in a famous Senate debate.

1831—William Lloyd Garrison begins publishing *The Liberator*.

1832—South Carolina rejects a federal tariff; President Andrew Jackson threatens to send federal troops to South Carolina to enforce the tax.

1833—Abolitionists form the American Anti-Slavery Society.

1837—Abolitionist publisher Elijah Lovejoy is murdered by a proslavery mob in Illinois.

1846—The Wilmot Proviso proposes that slavery be prohibited in the territories gained from Mexico.

1850—A new fugitive slave law, part of the Compromise of 1850, angers abolitionists.

1851 —Harriet Beecher Stowe publishes *Uncle Tom's Cabin*.
–1852

1854—The Kansas-Nebraska Act reopens Western territories to slavery and sets off a wave of violence in Kansas; The Republican party is formed.

1857—In the *Dred Scott* decision, the Supreme Court rules that Congress does not have the authority to bar slavery in the territories.

1859— Abolitionist John Brown leads a failed slave rebellion in Harpers Ferry, Virginia, and is executed for treason.

1860— *November*: Abraham Lincoln is elected president.
December 20: South Carolina secedes from the Union.

1861— *January 9–February 1*: Mississippi, Florida, Alabama, Georgia, Louisiana, Kansas, and Texas secede.
February: The seceding states draft the Confederate Constitution and name Jefferson Davis president.
March 4: President Lincoln is inaugurated.
April: Confederates fire on Fort Sumter in the opening battle of the Civil War; Virginia joins the Confederacy.
May: Arkansas and North Carolina secede; Richmond becomes the Confederate capital.
June: Tennessee secedes.
July 21: First Battle of Bull Run takes place.

1862— *March*: The *Monitor* and *Merrimack* are involved in the first engagement between ironclad ships.
April 6–7: Battle of Shiloh, Tennessee.
April 10–11: David Farragut captures New Orleans.
August 27–30: Second Battle of Bull Run takes place.
September: Confederate forces led by Robert E. Lee invade Maryland; Battle of Antietam takes place.
December 11–15: Battle of Fredericksburg, Virginia.

1863— *January*: Emancipation Proclamation goes into effect.
March: The United States government passes the first conscription act, drafting eligible men into military service; Antidraft riots break out in New York City.
April 30–May 6: Battle of Chancellorsville, Virginia.
May 22: United States General Ulysses S. Grant begins the siege of Vicksburg, Mississippi.
July 1: Battle of Gettysburg begins.
July 4: Vicksburg surrenders to the Union after a siege.
September 19–20: Battle of Chickamauga begins in Georgia.
November 19: President Abraham Lincoln dedicates a portion of the Gettysburg battlefield as a new national cemetery and delivers the Gettysburg Address.

1864—*May*: Battle of the Wilderness and Battle of Spotsylvania, Virginia, take place.
June: Battle of Cold Harbor, Virginia; Siege of Petersburg, Virginia, begins.
September 1: Atlanta surrenders to a Union Army force led by General William Tecumseh Sherman.
November: President Abraham Lincoln is elected to a second term.
December 23: Sherman's army captures Savannah, Georgia.

1865—*January 31*: Congress passes the Thirteenth Amendment to the Constitution, abolishing slavery in the United States, and submits it to the states for ratification.
February: Sherman's army marches through the Carolinas.
April: Lee's army evacuates Richmond and Petersburg; Lee surrenders to Grant at Appomattox Court House; President Lincoln is assassinated by John Wilkes Booth at Ford's Theatre in Washington, D.C.
May 23: Union troops are reviewed in Washington, D.C., and sent home; Reconstruction of the South begins.
December: Thirteenth Amendment to the Constitution is ratified.

★ CHAPTER NOTES ★

Chapter 1. War!

1. Geoffrey C. Ward, Ken Burns, and Ric Burns, *The Civil War* (New York: Alfred A. Knopf, 1990), p. 62.

2. Alan Nevins and Milton Halsey Thomas, eds., *The Diary of George Templeton Strong, Vol. III, 1860–1865* (New York: MacMillan, 1952), p. 169.

Chapter 2. Different Worlds

1. Mary Beth Norton et al., *A People and a Nation*, 3rd ed. (Boston: Houghton Mifflin, 1990), vol. 1, p. 336.

2. Ibid., p. 257.

3. Ibid., p. 245.

4. Ibid., p. 265.

5. Geoffrey C. Ward, Ken Burns, and Ric Burns, *The Civil War* (New York: Alfred A. Knopf, 1990), p. 12.

6. Norton et al., p. 10.

7. Ward et al., p. 14.

8. Ibid., p. 21.

9. Forest Wilson, *Crusader in Crinoline: The Life of Harriet Beecher Stowe* (Westport, Conn.: Greenwood Publishers, 1969), p. 484.

10. Andrew Carroll, ed., "A 'Dear Friend' to Harriet Beecher Stowe," *Letters of a Nation* (New York: Kodansha International, 1997), p. 103.

11. Norton et al., p. 358.

12. Craig Smith, *Defender of the Union: The Oratory of Daniel Webster* (New York: Greenwood Press, 1989), p. 165.

Chapter 3. A Nation Divided

1. Geoffrey C. Ward, Ken Burns, and Ric Burns, *The Civil War* (New York: Alfred A. Knopf, 1990), p. 14.

2. Philip S. Foner, *Business and Slavery: New York Merchants and the Irrepressible Conflict* (Chapel Hill, N.C.: University of North Carolina Press, 1941), p. 45.

3. "*Dred Scott* v. *Sanford*," *The Annals of America* (Chicago and London: Encyclopedia Britannica, Inc., 1976), vol. 8, p. 442.

4. Mary Beth Norton et al., *A People and a Nation*, 3rd ed. (Boston: Houghton Mifflin, 1990), vol. 1, p. 390; Ward et al., p. 22.

5. Ward et al., p. 26.

6. Ibid., p. 34.

Chapter 4. Life in the Union Army

1. Letter of Private Solomon Stocker, September 30, 1861, Camp Sutton, Virginia, to Julia Peter.

2. Bell Irvin Wiley, *The Life of Billy Yank: The Common Soldier of the Union* (Baton Rouge: Louisiana State University Press, 1997), p. 303.

3. Ibid., pp. 308–316.

4. J. Matthew Gallman, *The North Fights the Civil War: The Home Front* (Chicago: Ivan R. Dee, 1994), p. 67.

5. Letter of Stephen J. Wentworth, 4th N.H. Volunteers, Co. F, April 25, 1863, North Edisto, South Carolina.

6. Letter of Stephen J. Wentworth, 4th N.H. Volunteers, Co. F, December 24, 1861, Hilton Head, South Carolina.

7. Geoffrey C. Ward, Ken Burns, and Ric Burns, *The Civil War* (New York: Alfred A. Knopf, 1990), p. 127.

8. Letter of Stephen J. Wentworth, 4th N.H. Volunteers, Co. F, August 17, 1862, St. Augustine, Florida.

9. Gallman, p. 132.

10. Ward et al., p. 160.

11. Mary Beth Norton et al., *A People and a Nation*, 3rd ed. (Boston: Houghton Mifflin, 1990), vol. 1, p. 417.

12. Abraham Lincoln, "The Emancipation Proclamation," *Words That Make America Great*, ed. Jerome Agel (New York: Random House, 1997), p. 214.

13. Norton et al, p. 415.

14. Letter of Sergeant Samuel F. Hull, July 15, 1863, United States Military Hospital, West Philadelphia, to Emma Hull.

Chapter 5. The Home Front

1. Richard Bayles, *History of Windham County, Connecticut* (New York: W. W. Preston & Co., 1889), p. 100.

2. Mary Beth Norton et al., *A People and a Nation*, 3rd ed. (Boston: Houghton Mifflin, 1990), vol. 1, p. 414.

3. Reverend J. M. Stowe, *History of the Town of Hubbardston* (Gardner, Mass.: A. G. Bushnell, 1881), p. 146.

4. James Marten, *The Children's Civil War* (Chapel Hill: University of North Carolina Press, 1998), p. 180.

5. Catharine Hunsecker, "Civil War Reminiscences," *Franklin County Footnotes*, n.d., <http://jefferson.village.virginia.edu/vshadow2/KHS/hunsecker.html> (December 9, 1999).

6. Dorothy Denneen Volo and James M. Volo, *Daily Life in Civil War America* (Westport, Conn.: Greenwood Press, 1998), p. 162.

7. Letter of Stephen J. Wentworth, Co. F, 4th New Hampshire Volunteers, July 21, 1863, Morris Island, South Carolina, to Virginia Wentworth.

8. Walt Whitman, "A Missing Brother at Christmas," *Eyewitness to America: 500 Years of America in the Words of Those Who Saw It Happen*, ed. David Colbert (New York: Pantheon Books, 1997), pp. 236–237.

9. Clarence Bowen, *The History of Woodstock, Connecticut* (Somersworth: New Hampshire Printers Inc., 1973), pp. 353–369.

10. J. Matthew Gallman, *The North Fights the Civil War: The Home Front* (Chicago: Ivan R. Dee, 1994), p. 187.

Chapter 6. Struggling to Win

1. Letter of Sergeant Samuel F. Hull, 2nd R.I. Vols., May 22, 1863, 6th Corps Hospital, Sequia Creek Landing, to Emma Hull.

2. Letter of Private Solomon Stocker, 30th Ohio Volunteer Infantry, August 7, 1863, Camp Sherman, Mississippi, to Julia Peter.

3. Frank Petersohn, *10,000 Volkslieder, German and Other Folksongs,* 1996, <http://ingeb.org/songs/johnbrow.html> (May 10, 1999).

4. Frank Petersohn, *10,000 Volkslieder, German and Other Folksongs,* 1996, <http://ingeb.org/spiritua/mineyes.html> (May 10, 1999).

5. Letter of Stephen J. Wentworth, Co. F, 4th New Hampshire Volunteers, December 24, 1861, Hilton Head, South Carolina, to Charles Wentworth.

6. James M. McPherson, *Ordeal By Fire: The Civil War and Reconstruction* (New York: Alfred A. Knopf, 1982), p. 383.

7. Geoffrey C. Ward, Ken Burns, and Ric Burns, *The Civil War* (New York: Alfred A. Knopf, 1990), p. 236.

8. Sara M. Evans, *Born for Liberty: A History of Women in America* (New York: The Free Press, 1989), p. 114.

9. Letter of Private Solomon Stocker, 30th Ohio Volunteer Infantry, September 20, 1861, Sutton, Virginia, to Julia Peter.

10. Thomas A. Bailey and David M. Kennedy, *The American Spirit*, 6th ed. (Lexington, Mass.: D.C. Heath, 1987), vol. 1, p. 431.

11. Clarence Bowen, *The History of Woodstock, Connecticut* (Somersworth: New Hampshire Printers Inc., 1973), p. 358.

12. Letter of Stephen J. Wentworth, Company F, 4th New Hampshire Volunteers, December 12, 1861, Hilton Head, South Carolina.

13. Letter of Stephen J. Wentworth, Company F, 4th New Hampshire Volunteers, July 2, 1864, near Petersburg, Virginia, to Charles Wentworth.

14. Philip B. Kundhardt and Dorothy M. Kundhardt, *Twenty Days* (New York: Castle Books, 1993), p. 11.

15. Letter of Julia Peter, April 16, 1865, Gnadenhutten, Ohio, to Solomon Stocker.

Chapter 7. Reconstructing the Union

1. Geoffrey R. Stone, Louis M. Seidman, Cass R. Sunstein, and Mark V. Tushnet, "The Constitution of the United States," *Constitutional Law*, 2nd ed. (Boston: Little, Brown and Company, 1991), pp. lii–liii.

★ FURTHER READING ★

Books

Gaines, Ann Graham. *The Confederacy and the Civil War in American History*. Berkeley Heights, N.J.: Enslow Publishers, Inc., 2000.

Gallman, J. Matthew. *The North Fights the Civil War: The Home Front*. Chicago: Ivan R. Dee, Inc., 1994.

Kent, Zachary. *The Civil War: "A House Divided."* Hillside, N.J.: Enslow Publishers, Inc., 1994.

Marten, James. *The Children's Civil War*. Chapel Hill: University of North Carolina Press, 1998.

Volo, Dorothy Denneen, and James M. Volo. *Daily Life in Civil War America*. Westport, Conn.: Greenwood Press, 1998.

Ward, Geoffrey C., Ken Burns, and Ric Burns. *The Civil War*. New York: Alfred A. Knopf, 1990.

Whitelaw, Nancy. *Clara Barton: Civil War Nurse*. Springfield, N.J.: Enslow Publishers, Inc., 1997.

Wiley, Bell Irvin. *The Life of Billy Yank: The Common Soldier of the Union*. Baton Rouge: Louisiana State University Press, 1971.

Internet Addresses

American Civil War Home Page. February 24, 1995. <http://sunsite.utk.edu/civil-war/warweb.html> (May 7, 1999).

Civil War Page. n.d. <http://homepages.dsu.edu/jankej/civilwar/civilwar.htm> (November 23, 1999).

Library of Congress. *American Memory*. n.d. <http://lcweb2.loc.gov/ammem> (May 7, 1999).

★ INDEX ★